"Báyò Akómoláfé is a philosopher who is pushing us to think outside of every narrative we take for granted. In this text, he guides us to reconsider how we relate to the world—and to internalize the fact that earth and all of nature are alive, relating to us. *Selah* is an ancient Indigenous orientation, poured through Báyò's trickster poetry to make for a fresh agitation."
—ADRIENNE MAREE BROWN, author of *Pleasure Activism* and *Loving Corrections*

"There's a story about Borges, the great mischievous Argentinian writer, reading several books of Martin Buber and then discovering to his surprise that Buber was a philosopher. Why the surprise? Because Buber didn't make arguments. 'Arguments convince nobody,' Borges explained. 'But when something is merely said or—better still—hinted at, there is a kind of hospitality in our imagination.'

Báyò Akómoláfé is—among much else—a philosopher, but what I find in his work is this kind of imaginative hospitality. It opens itself up to everything that goes missing from our arguments, everyone who goes missing, all the ones who stray from the straight way and learn to dance with loss, to travel like rumors, to elude cognitive capture. *Selah* is a book full of invitations to the unmarked paths that branch off from the highway of progress. There's mischief waiting down those paths, and monstrous grace, and a poetry that unsettles all the assumptions we didn't even know we were making."
—DOUGALD HINE, author of *At Work in the Ruins*

"Like the carpenter ant sporulating cordyceps mushrooms from its forehead, one has the sense that Báyò Akómoláfé's insights might be dangerous to channel—that we are reading the final, perhaps fatal, fungal flourish of entities simultaneously too microscopic and too macrocosmic for our human organism to ever comprehend. These blessings do not offer protection. They offer divine infection—with mystery, with microbial anarchy, with revelry, and, most importantly, with a widened capacity for gardening in the ecotones of paradox. In a moment where there are no easy answers and no right side, Akómoláfé shows us how

to play in the fertile interstices between species, and how to pray in the fertile compost heap between sterile ideologies."
—SOPHIE STRAND, author of *The Body Is a Doorway* and *The Madonna Secret*

"As teetering border walls create glorious patterns of cracks and fissures in the architectures of certainty and loss, Báyò sweeps away the panicked grief of the Anthropocene with delight at the 'wondrous meanwhile' in which the world turns itself inside out and our edges migrate to the center of things. I often wonder why brother Báyò keeps engaging with me, when I spend all my time teasing thought leaders, or disrupting seekers of knowledge. Then I read *Selah* and understand that 'when wisdom becomes too full of itself, it needs the intervention of the stupid,' and that 'play is the poetics of the sideways.' Thus, as a fool/trickster, I am compelled to blurt out some spoilers and ruin the breathless anticipation of earnest readers: every standpoint has closets full of skeletons; the self is a multi-species collective; morality captures ethics just as games capture play; your identity, voice, and lived experience are artifacts of an illusory order imposed by the powerful; and empire seeks to colonize the world, but instead the colonized creolize the world. Each story and insight in *Selah* inducts us into the Möbius strip of brother Báyò's logic, compelling us not to seize on any of his words as truth, but to use his tools of peripheral cognition to follow the cracks and wounds of this world, to fully inhabit our entanglement."
—TYSON YUNKAPORTA, founder of the Indigenous Knowledge Systems Lab at Deakin University

"*Selah* is a thousand branching pathways, like the winding veins of rivers, blood, roots, and roads. As travelers we are invited to ride upside-down, to tilt and sway, to giggle and loosen the tyranny of expectation, tickling the familiar. As ossified ideas crumble in these pages, there is the possibility of ooze, and the ooze of possibility. Everything that once was said to be preferable is now not. Everything that once was taught to be foundational turns out to be illusion. We are called to upend the hallowed assumptions of modernity and drink the last drop of its hallucinations and then—with a great and revelatory bodily retch—behold

a crack, a peek into the world of vibrant relational swirls that have kept vigil for the ghosts of creation. Be ready to swallow your words, trip on your own feet, and forget your name. This book is important, it is a portal, a port from which to impart a new lostness. Thank you, Báyò, for unpeeling the petroleum pavement and releasing the muddy slime of poetic life."
—NORA BATESON, president of the International Bateson Institute and author of *Combining*

"In the 'right to opacity,' the com-post of post-activism gathers its more-than-human energies toward a politics of defamiliarization. Where blackness is how the cracks trouble the edifice of justice presupposed, bewilderment is cultivated. In care for how touch shifts the conditions of an earthly relation, in the tenderness of a grace 'that allows something different,' the struggle to ask the 'right' questions dances. No maps are provided in this lyrical unmaking of the time of white capture where 'to be embodied is to be beside oneself.'"
—DR. ERIN MANNING, Research Chair in Speculative Pragmatism, Art, and Pedagogy at Concordia University

Selah

Selah

A Báyò Akómoláfé Reader

Báyò Akómoláfé

Edited by Eden Pearlstein

Aora books are made possible through the generous support of Anne Germanacos and our grassroots donors and members. We are grateful for their dedication to transformational thought and culture that transcends borders, disciplines, and traditions.

Cover and book design by Melissa Weiss
Cover and book art by Krista Dragomer

Typeset in GT Super and Media Sans

First Edition
First Printing

Published by Aora Books, a sibling imprint of Ayin Press
Brooklyn, New York
www.aorabooks.org

Distributed by Publishers Group West, an Ingram brand
Printed in the USA

ISBN (paperback): 978-1-961814-31-8
ISBN (e-book): 978-1-961814-35-6

Library of Congress Control Number: 2025938638

Aora books may be purchased at a discounted rate by wholesalers, booksellers, book clubs, schools, universities, community organizations, and other institutions buying in bulk. For more information, please email *info@ayinpress.org*.

Follow us on social media *@AyinPress* and *@AoraBooks*.

Contents

INTRODUCTION
Selah: A Series of Ecstatic Irruptions

A revolt of... geologies, of scriptural things, of the heart.—But no commentaries! Poetry first!

—Paul Celan[1]

A *reader* is generally understood as referring to either one who reads (deeply), or a collection of writings focused on a particular author, theme, or field of inquiry. Books titled as "readers" tend to appear in scholarly settings as large and unwieldy tomes. A Marine Biology Reader, a Science Fiction Reader, a Decolonial Reader, a Marx Reader. If not quite exhaustive or encyclopedic, such readers are, at the very least, anthological attempts at being comprehensive. So what, then, is this slim and unobtrusive volume—and by what right does it refer to itself as a *reader*?

Some backstory may be helpful. I first came across Báyò's thought and writings in what I can only imagine is a comically common exchange: a friend of mine breathlessly sent me a short piece of Báyò's writing as if he had just offered me a sip from the holy grail; my friend had obviously already drunk the Kool-Aid, so to speak. I read it and liked it, but couldn't tell you exactly why or what it said or meant. But I did like it, and despite its brevity, a mélange of images and phrases continued to stick with me and pinball around my head. I was puzzled. Not that I was confused (though I most certainly was), but that I had, in some way, through this gnomic writing, been myself transformed into a puzzle, or been given a glimpse of the puzzling nature of reality writ large. When my friend asked me what I thought about Báyò's piece of

1 Paul Celan, *Letters to Gisèle* (New York Review Books, 2024), 191.

writing, I told them that I liked it, but that I didn't totally understand it. I asked them what they thought, and, truthfully, the more they tried to explain, the less I understood. And I liked that, too.

The resistance to collapse, capture, or paraphrase; the dense network of influences and interlocutors; the neologistic play and interdisciplinary promiscuity—in an age of algorithmic foie gras, when so much content is predetermined by the most predictable response rate, Báyò's writing and way of speaking seemed to disappoint every set expectation. It was not clear or concise or instantly accessible, it was rife with obscure references and specialized jargon from a range of fields, and yet it was avidly read and passionately discussed in both elite institutions and organically on- and offline among a growing tribe of unfamiliars—from artists to ecologists to (post)activists to Afrofuturists to neurodivergents of all stripes and none. Somehow, Báyò's writing finds a way to cross the blood-brain barrier.

And it is this very ability to escape, to hide, to stow away, to shapeshift that seems to me to be at the crux of Báyò's ontofugitive aesthetics and postactivist ethos. Born in Nigeria, raised in Germany and Congo, currently living with his family in India, and calling Brazil his spiritual home, Báyò is as close to a global citizen as I have personally encountered. And as an inheritor and translator of an equally polyvocal rhizome of stories and thought—from Karen Barad's agential realism to Jorge Ferrer's participatory spirituality, Jack Halberstam's queer art of failure to Yoruba trickster tales, Édouard Glissant's relational poetics to Gilles Deleuze's minor gestures, and so much more—Báyò has produced a body of work that feels increasingly labyrinthine, even Talmudic. It is oral and literate, with no clear point of entry. It is nonlinear, fractally intertextual, intergenerationally polyvocal, attuned to both the all-too- and more-than-human worlds, and obsessed with loopholes (or cracks, as Báyò refers to them). Where and how does one even begin to scratch such a surface without striating it?

One enters the world or the world enters you. Poetry engages.
—Wong May[2]

As interest in Báyò's idiosyncratic thought and writing has grown exponentially over the years—and with intercontinental awards, honors, and chairs accumulating—more people are asking this very same question. This *reader*, dear reader, is our attempt to provide just that: a place to begin—in the middle, of course. Such a project is not without its risks. How to construct an accessible collection that would satisfy neophytes and initiates alike; that would collect works from the past while offering something entirely new; that would introduce an array of Báyò's core concepts and concerns without collapsing the very real worlds they existed within; that would reject the well-intentioned but doomed-to-fail urge to simplify, streamline, and systematize for the sake of conceptual convenience?

The first piece of this puzzle came to me in the form of the book's title, which Báyò suggested at the beginning of our collaboration. *Selah*. A no-matter-how-familiar-still-mysterious word, which I knew from my studies of Hebrew philology and biblical poetics. The word appears seventy-four times throughout the Tanakh, almost exclusively in the Book of Psalms. Scholars have long debated the meaning of selah, with some suggesting that it is an exclamatory affirmation or signpost for thematic shifts in the flow of the psalms, while others claim it to be a kind of musical or choral notation, indicating a pause or break, a breath. In any case, selah is a meaningfully meaningless string of letters. A fertile void.

In Báyò's own words:

> *Selah is the name I give to the moment when understanding offers no more access, when language offers no usable description, when*

2 Wong May, "The Numbered Passages of a Rhinoceros in the China Shop," in *In the Same Light: 200 Poems for Our Century from the Migrants & Exiles of the Tang Dynasty* (The Song Cave, 2022), 283.

> *textuality falls off its pedestal, when the logic of continuity is momentarily bracketed by irruptions too powerful for the usual to have its way. I borrow the term, which is ambiguous and has had no fixed definition, from the ethnomusicological considerations of the Hebrew Bible. More than just a word for "contemplation," "turn it up," or "take a breather" (as suggested by those who propose that the term was used as a musical notation to tell musicians in the old palaces where they were to relax and pause, or raise their volume), selah's striking ambivalence seems fitting to the appearance of something "greater," something that derails convenient continuity. I therefore deploy the term as an ecumenical notation of sorts that is not to be reduced to its contested meanings.*

With all of this in mind, I began to read through thousands of pages of Báyò's books, articles, essays, social media posts, transcribed interviews, speeches, and lectures. It quickly became clear to me that besides being an exceptionally elastic thinker and fantastic writer in general, Báyò had a rare gift for the short form. Aphoristic blasts of poetic brilliance, lucid flashes smuggled into language. Philosophical fragments, prose poems, stuttering revelations, epistemological yoga postures. Interestingly, I found that these types of writing most often appeared in the informal forms of social media posts and micro essays published on Báyò's website. They had the air of the epiphanous about them, as if he were transcribing his thoughts as they occurred in real time. They were ecstatically lyrical and rigorously materialist at the same time. And they often contained the seeds of what would later grow into much more extensive long-form pieces of writing.

But these were something different. When I proposed to Báyò that we construct the reader entirely out of such short-form writings, and lay them out like prose poems that strung together to create a kind of book-length meditation, he took to it immediately. One long selah, composed of a series of smaller selahs—signaling to the reader that these were words/worlds meant to be entered into carefully, creatively, collaboratively.

Like prayer. Like art. Like play.[3]

"Selah," Báyò writes, "is the sweeping, shuddering blast of geo-philosophical winds from the monster's breath that render highways as crossroads. It is a call to touch, to trace, to fall together, to read together, to speculate about other forms of care. Beyond salvation and submission, there is the still small voice—selah."

And now, without further ado,
we present this *reader* to you,
dear reader.

—Eden Pearlstein, May 2025[4]

---

3 My editorial approach was guided by the aphoristic adepts Walter Benjamin, who wrote, "Work on good writing has three steps: a musical phase when it is composed, an architectural phase when it is built, and a textile phase when it is woven," and Jalal Toufic, who wrote a half century later, "An aphoristic book requires from its author the perforation of walls for the reception of aphorisms, and demands from its reader quantum tunneling between the consecutive aphorisms."

4 Immense gratitude goes out to Adam Segulah Sher and Daisy Crane, without whose vision, support, and friendship this book would not exist.

Selah

•

If you can get a handle on it, it's probably a door.
I'm wary of doors.
And doorways.

Doors are anticipated architectural technologies. They grant access, they permit exits. What's critical to note about doors is that they maintain the logic of the architectural frame. A building does not lose its integrity with the inclusion of a door. Doors are systemic agents granting mobility within familiar fields. As such, like the solutions we often offer to our most persistent civilizational challenges, doors allow us to shuffle within the already-known, to move the pieces around in the name of innovation, while maintaining the design.

Doors "behave."

You know what doesn't "behave"? Cracks. Architects don't design cracks, don't anticipate cracks. Cracks are not part of the furniture; they are the excessiveness of the frame. Design's ecstasy. They are neither external nor internal. Cracks are not "solutions," not guarantees or final answers. But something about them marks deterritorializing tensions, and obliquely traces out new realities.

•

•

In 1897,[1] British troops burned the city of Benin (in present day Nigeria) and its inhabitants to the ground, imprisoned the king, and looted treasures from the king's palace to avenge the killing of British officials by the natives. James Phillips, one of the officials in question, was headed to Oba Ovonramwen's palace—even though he had been warned against doing so during a time of sacred rituals. Phillips and others in his company were killed. The Empire's reprisal was swift, and the city was reduced to an ashen heap of mere nothings. Mind you, Benin City wasn't a collection of huts: it was said to have walls more fortified than the Chinese Wall, and the earliest form of street lights. The pilfered "treasures" from the palace—elaborate carvings, metal sculptures, figurines, tusks, an ivory mask, and art from five hundred years ago—made their way across the British Empire and to 161 museums, mostly in the "West," over the next century: the British Museum, Berlin's Humboldt Forum, the Metropolitan Museum of Art in New York, the Art Institute of Chicago, the Los Angeles County Museum of Art, the Victoria and Albert Museum in London, the Jacques Chirac Museum of Branly Quay in Paris, the Vatican Museums, the Australian Museum in Sydney, the National Museum of Ethnology in Osaka, and the Louvre Abu Dhabi in the United Arab Emirates. Two of those artifacts also made their way to the home of one Mark Walker, grandson of Captain Herbert Walker, who was part of the Benin Punitive Expedition—the force of five hundred men that would leave one of Africa's greatest cities "littered with sculls [*sic*] and corpses."

---

1 On January 2, 1897, British Acting Consul-General James Robert Phillips had set out to meet the Oba of Benin, against the wishes of the king's court. His ill-fated journey, which ended with the ambush and killing of much of his delegation by local Edo groups who probably acted independently of the Oba's wishes, sparked off the events that led to the devastating punitive response by the British Empire—the destruction of the Kingdom of Benin and the pilfering of its precious art as the spoils of war.

"The Raid on Benin, 1897," National Museum of African Art, Smithsonian Institution, accessed March 10, 2025, https://africa.si.edu/exhibitions/current-exhibitions/visionary-viewpoints-on-africas-arts/the-raid-on-benin-1897/; "The British Conquest of Benin and the Oba's Return," *Benin—Kings and Rituals: Court Arts from Nigeria*, Art Institute of Chicago, accessed March 10, 2025, https://archive.artic.edu/benin/conquest/; *Dahomey*, directed by Mati Diop (France, Senegal, and Benin, 2024).

Old man Mark Walker had inherited those two artifacts, and did not know what they were. He did not know they were our ancestors. He recalled his grandmother using one of them as a door stopper; they were handy that way. One day, after going through his grandfather's journal notes, he decided to return the items.

In his well-publicized adventure back to the world his grandfather had helped destroy, Walker arrived in Benin, meeting great anger, red eyes, and sharpened axes. I'm kidding. Perhaps, that was what he expected to meet. Instead, the Benin people threw a huge party for him, welcoming him with open arms—the son of he who had killed their own fathers and mothers. Then Dr. Walker gave back the two seemingly insignificant "door stoppers," receiving even more pieces of art in return to take home with him. Walker was surprised, recounting later in an interview that he had not expected to return to England with a larger suitcase than he left with.

But there's more to this story: the other stolen artifacts that settled in museums in Europe and America started to, well, "do" things. In a 2020 investigation published by *The Economist*, written and researched by Killian Fox, and titled "Are Ghosts Haunting the British Museum?," museum staff reported "inexplicable noises, spectral sightings, [and] sudden drops in temperature" around the art pieces. They would chain certain doors shut after visiting hours, retreat to their offices—only to see those doors unfastened and wide open when they made their inspection rounds. The author concluded, "something strange is going on at the British Museum." What may have seemed like the final resting place for these objects was anything but. The objects haunted their "masters," resisting absolute capture, littering the place with ontological filth, refusing to sit still.

You see, when the learned conveners of the term "cultural appropriation" made their scholarly observation, they did so using the onto-epistemological-ethical resources of the world they knew, the modern rationalistic world they understood. It was a useful strategy for naming the insidious encroachments of dominant powers, the uneven territories of cultural "exchange." What these well-intentioned guilds of thought did not count on was a world in which things ... do things. A world that cannot be fully "appropriated" or "captured"—a world in which "to take" is also "to be taken by."

In this sense, popular notions of cultural appropriation, derived from modern examinations of culture, rendered with striation marks of progressivism, fail to convene the decolonial sense of what Jane Bennett calls "thing power." While composed of fine-sounding sentiments and gestures, the general concept of cultural appropriation fails to account for the agency of the more-than-human, and thus reinforces an ethical edifice that reproduces the problematic "brutal humanism" (Jasbir Puar) that is now considered the heart of the Anthropocene. Even more critically, applications of the charge of cultural appropriation willy-nilly fail to comprehend or account for the remarkable generosity of my people—including the cosmological instigations that would lead them to celebrate a descendant of their enemies.

Pat McCabe expresses it beautifully when she says that there is a need for a canny intelligence that knows the trickster's ways. That the rationalism and puritanism of our dominant culture leave us stuck in a hopeless naïveté, completely unable to detect or to match this trickster energy in creation. That is, the puritan ethical response of contemporary activism and conscientiousness cannot meet the overwhelming demands (or rise to the occasion) of transformation.

•

•

Think about it: the force of deep time, eons of uncalendared years—nameless and frothing at the turbulent edges of the cosmos—rolling on and on. Spinning and spinning. Exploding stars. Supernovae. Matter mattering. Coagulatory forces birthing planets and stellar bodies. The cosmos dancing though billions and billions of years in testy negotiations with the unspeakable. And then all that spinning arrives at the production of something tender: the papery skin of a seed coat. The stentorian outrage of a quasar detonation falling to its knees, gently, to protect a fragile embryo from adverse ecological forces.

Something about the mighty stooping to the delicate requires a different logic, a different way of thinking about origins and becomings. Perhaps the physics doesn't add up, but I would argue that it takes more energy for the universe to alchemize the soft skin of a seed than it does to sprout a black hole.

Now consider how this exquisite production—the genius of billions of nameless years—is, in an instant, imploded and cracked open in the depths of the earth. You would think the hard-won victory of galvanizing unwieldy forces to produce something so ethereal would suggest the need for safety. Security measures of some kind. On the contrary, the very same universe that manufactures the textural equivalent of a whisper summarily destroys it in the heat of the loam.

Why does the universe do this?

We hardly notice it in this way but loss is the most delicate creation of the universe. Its most exquisite art. A carrier bag of new fictions might pick loss up, moist and soft from the earth, and give it a pride of place among the war-exhausted narratives about how new things come to be. Loss needs a new cosmology—a minor gesture that touches the sapling in the soot of demise. Loss needs a new cosmology: not one that treats it as a deficit, something to fill quickly with a replacement; nor as sustainability—the disguised primal cry of the modern self in search of permanence.

Loss needs a new home. Suitably, one that wanders.

•

•

Regeneration does its best work, I would suppose, not as a sign of clumsy replacements of lost things, a sprouting into empty space of an iteration of what was previously taken—as would be the case if we imagined the world to be composed of stable things that occasionally go missing. Within such an ontology, a world of infinite growth and progressive capture, absence is problematic—a void to be filled. Like Death to the author of Revelation: a final enemy to be vanquished. In this world, regeneration fits into an economy of named things, of saved things, accommodated within our systems, proper only to the extent that it serves "us."

But doesn't loss have a hidden life? A secret fermenting in its body like a fungal parasitoid in the chest of an insect? At what point does grieving become the choreography of a strange joy? Maybe loss is also infected. Infected with becoming. Maybe we need to think of loss in more fruitful ways. Maybe loss needs a new ontology. Maybe regeneration does its best work ... as a call to worship.

•

•

There are stowaway worlds tucked into the dense folds of the ordinary. Hidden lives, secret celebrations. Appliances conversing with each other when we've gone to sleep. Dolphins arguing about which experimental modality is more appropriate for studying the human that researches them. Spider cognitions braided into the arachnean corners of a decrepit apartment. Slave bones humming freedom beneath the asphalt of a post-racial utopia. Gut bacterial families whispering their desire to our brains. A zombie—the forbidden child of the crossroads, born at the site where empire meets magic—lurks at the peripheries of the modern. We can never be sure of what the world is doing next, what it is producing, what lines are being blurred, what categories are being composted. If we do not cultivate bewilderment, we will risk seeing things too clearly in a world and at a time when clarity often gets in the way.

•

•

A dry, browning, withering leaf still attached to the stem sustains marcescent relations with its tree. “Marcescence” names arboreal practices in which fading leaves no longer draw nourishment from their trees, and yet are kept in place, mesmerized in their wilting, unable to fall away as winter howls its piper’s tune.

Something about marcescence hints at dominant practices, especially in justice-oriented movements, of seeking greater freedoms, greater expressibility, greater access, or greater representations within relations that no longer nourish. Within epistemologies that incarcerate futures. When this happens, when our labors are concerned exclusively with seeking more “freedom,” we risk fortifying marcescent dynamics. We risk reproducing patterns that exceed the immediacy of resolutions.

Transformative differences may not always be tied to seeking greater freedoms or greater stability within familiar worlds. Quite to the contrary, it would seem that it is in the falling away, the descending, and the waltzing to the earth, that potential new worlds unfurl.

Cracks portend some kind of crossroads captivity: one has to be carried away, shapeshifted, crossed out, and “taken.” From the perspective of marcescent freedom, this falling away might look like pathology, like something to be fixed, like an unfortunate deviation from proper society. But there’s perhaps nothing more promising to the otherwise, to the prospects of new subjectivities than a leaf that has fallen off its branch. The monstrosity of a fallen leaf, torn away from its tree, is a prophecy of forests yet to come.

•

•

During flight turbulence, the captain turns on the "fasten seat belt" sign. The blinking lights intone a warning. If atmospheric pressure persists, the captain makes an announcement: "Flight attendants please be seated." But you know things have gone horribly wrong when everyone is asked to "brace for impact"!

Bracing is a postural response to turbulence that exceeds aeronautical events. There is a sense in which bracing, a grasping for fixity, a two-armed turning-away-from-the-outside and a turning-to-oneself, defines an increasingly globalized response to civilizational trouble.

Bracing is a hardening of positionality in the face of corrosive inflections. It is thinking like a dot while overwhelmed in a murmuration of lines. Bracing names the stupefaction of conventional, normopathic politics: an uncritical emphasis on safety and trigger warnings in the North; an insistence on catch-up imperatives and growth in the South. A deification of uniformity. A vilification of nuance.

Bracing is how the public forces us to stay put, to occupy the seats in metal flight, to focus on arriving, to secure ourselves first before anyone else. To keep our heads fastened to their necks against the whiplash of a bad landing.

But arriving intact is difficult to do if we are already spread out. If we are not fully named or fully designated. There's a name for civilizational demise and the politics it invites, one which "bracing" attempts to postpone: grace.

•

•

In our familiar songs, grace is amazing, comely, beautiful, and acceptable. I think otherwise, as do our histories of encountering the foreign, the stranger. Because grace forces new considerations, reformulates positionalities, and disrupts familiar modes of thinking. In other words: grace is necessarily monstrous.

Grace is out of the question, beside the point, and unwieldy. Grace is awkward, ugly, messy, the irrupted tensions within an exhausted moral system.

If grace were to show up on our streets, we'd lock it up because it would spoil the business of the day. And yet, therein—in its uncomeliness and monstrosity—lies its promise. The thing to do, when grace comes piercing through, is to risk touching it, to risk welcoming it into our homes, to risk washing its feet.

Somewhere in the curdled middle of accompanying this stranger called grace, we might find a prior generosity, an unpronounceable hope, a sudden opening in the wooden closures of the stolen night, a gift tucked between the repulsive scales of the dragon we refused to slay.

•

•

I will tell you a story now.

At first the gods pitied the tortoise, known in Yoruba folklore as Ijapa, when he rudely declared before their divine council that he could know "everything" there was to know about the world. They pitied him as the ocean pities a little frothing wave wanting to be as big as the ocean. They rolled their eyes, smacked their lips, and hissed. And not even in the polite way that our parents taught us to hide our disgust from its object. But then their pity slowly metastasized into a creeping worry as the redoubtable reptile stood his ground. Nothing they did or said to wean the rocking head of the tortoise from its destructive confidence could move him. Resigning themselves to their failure, they sent him on his way, urging him to try his luck.

True to form, Ijapa swung into action. He purchased for himself a gourd with a slender neck and a fat belly, tied a string to the thing, and left his home on an adventure to articulate his final theory of everything.

And so began Tortoise's quest to know everything once and for all. He met with Lion and asked her about her roar. How she did it. How she made it tremble and stretch out into the forest. When she opened her mouth to demonstrate the ferociousness of her pride, he took the information from the air with his magic and stuffed it into his gourd. Before the day was done, Tortoise had interviewed Tiger, Giraffe, Hippo, Man, Tree, Mountain, River, Sky, Moon, Sun, and Star. Each one donated a piece of its wisdom to Tortoise's gourd, which the old trickster promptly secured with his buckskin and string.

When a week of four days was over, Tortoise knew everything. His gourd simmered, glowed, and trembled with a strange engorgement. Believing himself to now be the wisest of all creatures, Tortoise decided to hide his invaluable treasure away from prying eyes and jealous gods. He chose the Iroko tree, proud and tall, for the assignment. "I will climb to the height of this tree," said Tortoise to himself, "and camouflage my gourd amongst its rich foliage."

Wrapping his limbs a fraction of the way around the stubborn trunk of the tree, Tortoise's final lap soon proved more difficult than he had anticipated. No matter how hard he tried to get a grip, the tree resisted his abbreviated embrace. Nevertheless, the intoxication of the glowing gourd, hanging on his chest by a string, did not dim or grow faint. His eyes, swirling with the arousal for his beloved, were red with passion. He had traveled the entire cosmos in a week. Now at the foot of a mere tree, he was not to be stopped by a few muscular disadvantages—he, the conqueror of Thought itself!

In a bush nearby, the grasshopper—often considered the stupidest of all animals—watched Ijapa and his gourd. He wasn't bothered at first. There were better things to do than to watch the old fool fall flat on his face again and again. But it is often the case that when wisdom becomes too full of itself, it needs the intervention of the stupid to release it from the tyranny of its presumptions.

So, Grasshopper hopped out to the Tortoise, startling him.
"My friend!" Grasshopper bellowed. "What is it you are up to?"
Irritated by such a disreputable interruption, Tortoise grunted his disapproval. "Say what you want, trifling, and be on your way. This is none of your business."

Grasshopper seemed to be in thought for a while, and then he smiled. "I am sorry to bother you, wise friend. You see, I have been watching you try to climb this tree." He began to hop away. "Why don't you put the gourd around your back? See if that helps." And without further ado, Grasshopper skipped away.

The realization hit Tortoise harder than the time Elephant had slapped him away from a bowl of porridge at Hippo's house. Or the time he had leapt from the clouds—at a gathering hosted strictly for the birds—towards a small heap of sharp objects gathered on the ground.

Grasshopper's stupidity was equal to his archival mastery!

Of what use was it to own all knowledge when the merest of beings had won in a battle of wits? Perhaps there was no such thing as a final approximation of the world. Perhaps the idea of the world as a stable containment of pieces of insights that could be captured and fully controlled was itself a limited modality that excluded and obscured the promiscuously deep relationality implied in any act of knowing. Perhaps there was no stable content to be gained—and Grasshopper's stupidity, the dissonant quality of his happy-go-lucky ways, was wise in relation to his rigid attempts at containment. Perhaps wisdom itself was a thorn in the flesh, the cautionary finger-wag of a world that could not be known by one name.

Tortoise was already halfway up the tree, the gourd resting on his geometric shell, when he began to ponder the irony of his folly. When he reached the top of the Iroko tree, the clouds and the stars collected each other in a spiral in the heavens, heralding the irresistible arrival of the gods, who had come to see the end of Tortoise's ritual. With his head hung low, Tortoise unsheathed the string from the neck of the gourd and tossed away the skin that held everything together. In small melodic morsels of light, like fireflies floating in procession, the gourd's contents floated back into the world.

•

•

Wisdom is what remains when we've come to the end of everything we know.

Wisdom is not something we own, not a property of selves. It is an enlistment; an impersonal territorial asundering of bodies in their knowledge-making practices; a transversal crossing-through of the steady parallelity of the normal path. Like a saffron comet piercing the uneven obsidian of the night sky.

Wisdom is the place where the world kicks back, where something that resists the instrumentality of common sense bursts open and spills through—making a way.

•

•

I used to think the miraculous indexed a rarity, the wondrous point where a transcendent being tinkers with the bovine goings-on and ordinariness of the world. Physics momentarily suspended; walls of water frozen in mid-spill; dry bones coming together to live again. Now I think otherwise: the miraculous is not the stunning exception to the quotidian rule. Neither is it the rule without exception. The miraculous is located in the relations that permit us to notice that the rule is still being made, is never finished, never complete, never fully rendered, never fully available, neither fully rule nor exception.

The miraculous is a paradigm. Ask the zombie ant in mid-flight; wonder at the phantom lives of *Pfiesteria piscicida*; watch an autistic son who, while drawing circles with his shuffling feet, says to his father: "There are certain things I have to do that you don't know about."

•

•

Play is uncircumscribed, spilling beyond frameworks. Indeed, it is the restlessness of the frame. When we build walls around play, we create games. But it is an unfortunate irony of our modern moment that we seem to have a lot of games and no room for play.

Much has been written about the utility of play, perhaps—most especially—its importance in the lives of growing children. Very little, it would seem, is written about the uselessness of play. The utility of play is easier to talk about, easier to build into curricula, easier to render into standards, easier to centralize, easier to spell.

Something is however lost in the grammar of usefulness. Once "play" moves away from the margins and becomes important, it becomes less itself. Perhaps then, quite paradoxically, play cannot be conceived completely within our systems that allocate significance and worth and value. Something about play spills beyond utility, refuses ontological traps, cannot be scaled up, lingers in the margins, thrives in the minor, emancipates through underground passageways of the useless.

Play is the poetics of the sideways, how ontologies are beside themselves.

•

•

"Being" is not the substrate of "becoming." There are no elite foundations. There are no summits to this climbing that are not already bridges to elsewheres; there are no valleys to arrive at that do not spill into otherwises. There are no ultimates that are not already penultimate. The edges are in the middle, in this wondrous meanwhile. And we must learn to live and yearn and think here.

•

•

Gbogbo alangba lo d'anu dele, a ko mo eyi t'inu nrun.

This is a Yoruba proverb that translates as: "All lizards lie flat on their stomachs and so it is difficult to determine which has a stomachache."

In these moments, what the proverb really wants to do is invite a posture of hesitation about the convenient judgments we make about others. The proverb invites us to see others less as fixed standpoints on a spectrum of correctness, and more as moving lines, yearning gestures, middling strategies, ecosystems of contradiction, and non-reductionistic agonistic forces without resolution.

What today's increasingly tribalized, puritanical, dialogic spaces know how to do well is produce stable objects of critique. We are being habituated into seeing the "other" as a finished product, a stable self with beliefs, practices, thoughts, attitudes, and ideas that can be measured against "the correct answer," the right moral stance, the right thing to say.

What might change if we were allowed the gift of noticing that even standpoints, however monumental, have hidden lives? That bodies are never stable, but are instead fluid becomings that cannot be reduced to the images proliferated by modernity? What might change if we were invited to sit still with the simple and yet troublingly profound idea that none of us has figured out how to live and none of us will?

Might a stranger compassion take us then? Might it become easier for us to offer the project of our lives—the living of which no one seems to have gained expertise in—to the village of others with whom we've always shared our days?

•

•

By Hesiod's reckoning, when the void touched itself with orgasmic desire, out sprang Chaos—the first being to emerge from the enthused deep. It was Chaos that summoned the primordial beings, Gaia and Uranus, earth and sky, mother and father of everything else to come. In time, Gaia would give birth to the Titans, the pantheon of gods, the Cyclopes, and monsters of different kinds. But of all her children, none were as justifiably feared or as fantastically formidable as the dreadful Hecatoncheires: Briareus, Cottus, and Gyges—three giant monsters with a hundred arms and fifty heads, each.

The Hecatoncheires were so terrifying to behold that Uranus imprisoned them, locking them away in Tartarus until, in another version of the tale, Gaia and Cronus freed them—only for the latter to reincarcerate the beasts, an incident that would later prove fatal to the Titans in their battle for cosmic supremacy against Zeus and the Olympians. With the terrifying Hundred-Handed Ones on their side—with Cottus and Gyges uprooting and hauling entire mountains, and Briareus stealing the wind from the throats of his adversaries just by showing up—the Olympians fought off the Titans and brought the Titanomachy to an end. Zeus would later reward the three horrifying brothers with a new role: guardians of the gates of Tartarus.

But there was a fourth member of the Hecatoncheires, less talked about than the others, his story buried under sediments of sand and fade. He is mentioned neither by Hesiod nor by Homer, and he didn't fight alongside his brothers in the Titanomachy.

Purveyors of darker fables suggest this forgotten Hecatoncheir slept through time, through ages and legends, through kingdoms won and lost, through empires built and abandoned, until he was awakened by the din of industry, the harsh cacophonies of metallic vehicles plotting feverish cartographies on the flesh of his back. Awakened by the rush of the modern.

Seeing his back was as vast as the outdoors, and his girth as wide as their ambitions, the city leaders put the orphaned Hecatoncheir to work: "Just like your old brothers," they said, "you must guard the entrances of the city. Guard them so that no one might leave. Protect us.

"Carry us away from the captivity of our bodies and their swirling migrancies; from the elements beneath us—the swindling deceit of death. Lift us high above the ground so we can aspire to the heights where we belong. Allow us to lay railway tracks along your spine; to tattoo your surface with the spells and rituals of power.

"Let the stretch of your torso be the distance between despair and justice. And let the traversing of that distance be the measure of hope.

"Give the citizens a place to protest their pains somewhere on the sprawl of your chest, close to one of your many heads, so they do not lose sight of where power lies. So that they covet the privilege of standing on your heads.

"In return," they said, "we will massage your flesh with our goings and comings, and ease the pain of centuries inflicted on your necks."

The Hecatoncheir obliged, and became "the City." The citizens in return repaid his good work by giving him a name: Demosios.

Meaning "the public."

•

•

The public is not a simple location, not a "place" nestled entirely within stable coordinates. Not a mere chalice or an orphaned container holding humans in their busy mobilities. Not a background to the theater of human sociality. Instead, the public is an imperative, a field of roaming intensities that convenes and composes bodies in their open-ended becomings.

We might suppose that when "we" move through "the city"; navigating its networks; braiding its sidewalks with hustling feet; reading chalked menus hastily slapped on windows; stopping at red lights and exhaling when they turn green; and, generally, shuffling from here to there, the "we" making these movements refers to complete, autonomous, self-directed individuals simply moving past a background of noise. But there is no pre-relational "we" in any independent sense. No intact identities moving atomically through Brownian fluids.[2] The concrete walls and asphalt roads and neon-lit signs around us are social actors with compositional powers. We are made in the interstitial loops and stitched in the creative inquiry of the public, which is always more-than-human.

•

2 Brownian motion in fluids is the random, chaotic movement of particles suspended in a fluid due to the bombardment of surrounding molecules. "Brownian Motion," ScienceDirect, accessed March 10, 2025, https://www.sciencedirect.com/topics/physics-and-astronomy/brownian-motion.

•

We often speak about creativity as if it were a human thing, a matter of souls and their interior arpeggiations; a matter of isolated and independent individuals and their gilded geniuses; a matter of "talents" or hard work. Like Narcissus entranced by his own reflection in a pool of water, we suppose that the proper subject of creativity is the absolute self. From this presupposition, we anticipate that we can imagine ourselves out of our gridlock impasses.

But selves are not isolated objects in space; selves are entanglements of place-time. Selves are ecological propositions, meandering temporalities, geological musings, and multispecies arrangements. The individual is already a crossroads. When Jean-Marc Côté was commissioned to imagine the year 2000 in 1899, the images he produced—of flying vehicles and automated machines and their queerly fashioned operators—strikingly resembled the world he occupied. Those images were 1899's "Year 2000"; they were the speculative virtualities of Jean-Marc's thick present. Today, you might be able to notice tautological patterns in everything from how we tell stories to how we design movie trailers, how we compose agency and political action, how we dress ourselves up, how we design cars, and how we imagine the future.

The hypothetical year 3000 probably evokes in you either a dystopic world of rust and red-clawed trans-cyborgian-human tribes or, perhaps, lingers along the lines of utopian settlements, phallic towers silhouetted by a sun we can now control. Whatever it is, the images are not two-dimensional secretions of your "independent" mind, but shared molecular inquiries that connect bacteria, viruses, fungal entities, architectural arrangements, and more-than-human materials. In short, imagination is not human per se; creativity is a matter of naturecultures,[3] which churn, think, yearn, and bleed—together. Non-localized rhizomatic processes that incarcerate, close in upon, cleave apart, and reconstitute—in and for a fleeting moment.

The kinds of creativities we need today are bound up in new alliances, new gestures, new cognitions, new fidelities, new gut bacteria, new infections, new kinds of gastronomic adventures, new shadows, new failures.

•

3 "Natureculture is a synthesis of nature and culture that recognizes their inseparability in ecological relationships that are both biophysically and socially formed. Natureculture is a concept that emerges from the scholarly interrogation of dualisms that are deeply embedded within the intellectual traditions of the sciences and humanities (e.g., human/animal; nature/culture)." Nicholas Malone and Kathryn Ovenden, "Natureculture," in *The International Encyclopedia of Primatology*, ed. Agustín Fuentes (Wiley-Blackwell, 2017), https://doi.org/10.1002/9781119179313.wbprim0135. See also: Agustín Fuentes, "Naturalcultural Encounters in Bali: Monkeys, Temples, Tourists, and Ethnoprimatology," *Cultural Anthropology* 25, no. 4 (2010): 600–624, https://doi.org/10.1111/j.1548-1360.2010.01071.x; and Donna J. Haraway, *The Companion Species Manifesto: Dogs, People, and Significant Otherness* (Prickly Paradigm Press, 2003).

•

I find the presupposition that "artificial intelligences" are "artificial"—namely, the idea that humans have "natural intelligence"—to be more consequential, more interesting, than any of the many forecasts of an impending AI totalitarian takeover.

There's a subtle ontological move crystallized in the attribution of "artificiality": a subtlety that works as an apartheid system, which is now playing out in anxious efforts to reassert our dominance and exclusivity. "Well, AI can mimic us, but it can't really do poetry." "ChatGPT can do essays, but it isn't wise." "Oh no, the livelihoods of artists and animators are threatened by the emergence of AI."

At some level, the panic is justified: deepfakes, quasi-sentient bots, and artistic algorithms effectively trouble "our" vaunted place in the scheme of things. It's difficult to know what to do here, to know what to do with artificiality. Perhaps one thing to do is to trouble the assumption of distance between the artificial and the natural.

Maybe nature is unnatural. Maybe nature is artificial. Maybe artifice has a hidden life, the kind that the legendary animators of the *Toy Story* series transcribed to our delight ... the kind theologians of panentheistic persuasions wax poetic about. Maybe this is an instance of excess, where something decidedly modern spills beyond itself, becomes fugitive, and calls into question the corporeal forms we've adopted.

Maybe we are all AI. And maybe we are not. All at once. Maybe we are all together a part of the frothing foliage of emergence that does not allocate intelligence in a fixed manner.

•

•

The earth is not a stable thing, a principled location locked into the subservience of playing backstage to human mobility. Instead, the earth is moving. And "it" is moving so irreverently that one might say the planet is becoming fugitive. That's why the cracks are showing up everywhere: cracks in settlement; cracks in neurotypicality; cracks in human exclusivity; cracks in democracy and the legitimacy of the nation-state; cracks in time; cracks in being.

I am convinced—in the creaturely ways that conviction marks a gesturing towards and a yearning in risky directions—that this loss of stability, this ontofugitivity of things, traces out a geophilosophy that invites a reconsideration of the premises that have conditioned experience, articulated civilizational problems, and instigated resolutions. Cracks become matters of ontogenesis, intercessory sites of what is to come and what is not quite done-with. We need a geophilosophy that cultivates ways of following cracks to where they might lead.

•

•

A crack is a rift in the fabric of spacetime, a sacred moment. It is sacred because it hints at the ongoing mobility of "all" things, and suggests that our image of the world, our images of white modernity, of capitalism, of slavery, of justice, of the future, of anything at all, are not static representations of something "objectively" true, but relationships of placemaking and worlding that have risks.

What this means is that what we, for instance, name and lionize as "modernity" doesn't refer to a fixed reality outside our sensemaking practices. Modernity is made up in part by our social analytics, by instigations in the environment, by things we are doing and things the world is doing to us. Modernity is a relationship, a social production. When we critique it, we are pointing out the ways our analysis of the world discloses to us the inadequacies of a social arrangement, how it for instance uses black and brown bodies as props, how it enlists white bodies as avatars of purity and ascension, how it doesn't grant us all stable grounds to stand upon.

However, we can very often get stuck in images: by treating modernity as a thing to be dismantled, dismissed, destroyed, we become so affixed to its "thingness" that we lose sight of how we are participating within "it," how even critique is a form of worldmaking that has preservative qualities. Images are never still. Indeed, by focusing on a thing as an image (in this instance, modernity), we obscure the ways "it" is changing, becoming different, never quite static, often beside itself, desirous of something else.

And this is what thinking along with cracks (going into cracks) allows us to do: to cultivate an aliveness and animacy that allow us to follow those delicate moments of spillage, when—to keep up with our example—modernity doesn't quite behave like itself. When modernity "fails" to keep up with itself.

•

•

None of us have it down; none of us can hold it together. We are the frothing, feathery edges of an explosion that is still fanning out into its own creases.

—

They often say that there is no air in outer space. But isn't it remarkable that it is in those moments when I think of far-flung galaxies beyond the anxieties of survival, or the blackening mysteries of the expanse that stretches beyond the sonic playgrounds of Saturn's rings, and the terrifying roar of a black hole awakened by a cloud of dust—isn't it something that it is in these moments that I really breathe?

—

Morality is ethics captured. First, ethics is flow, the ongoing drunken dance of the cosmos in its ephemeral immanence. In its differentiation from itself. What comes to matter (that is, how the material world becomes itself, or ontology) can be conceived as a matter of ethics. A mighty flow. A river.

Periodically, this dance of ethics circles around itself, spins on its axis, and then coagulates into a solid. Into laws and precepts. Into ideas of good and evil. Into fundamentalisms that pretend to be anchored to something deeper than the murky, loamy movement of things. Like an ice cube bobbing along in a river.

Morality is thus born of arrangements, of moving things which counterfeit stability. We are "good" or "bad" only within these dense fields of relations. Further still, the circuitous motions within these seemingly stable architectures become so impervious to other flows, other possibilities, other events, that they start to hollow out. When things get too solid, when being good preserves an architecture that does nothing more than asserting its own primacy, then cracks emerge … with a monstrous proposal: becoming sensuous. The ice cube is unable to sustain its solidity. The edges rupture, spill. And its organelles rejoin the riverine flow of things already coalescing into other shapes.

—

The premises of peace are not founded on who's correct.

•

•

When the world becomes too solid for nuance, when it hardens up and crystallizes into a binary that forces you to pick a side, compelling you to become intelligible to the hardness that creeps on its once loamy surfaces, cracks become the first responders.

We need a politics of tenderness more than ever. Not tenderness as capitulation to particular conclusions that have already been made. Not tenderness as in, "If you don't see the world as I do, there's something wrong with you." But tenderness as the nurturance of grace that allows something different, something even beautiful, to be born in the midst of the fires that surround and engulf us.

•

•

An obstacle is the richest, thickest, densest place in the universe. This is so because it is where things stop and often die, failing to continue on their way. It is where carcasses of hope rot into the ground, inadvertently fertilizing the earthly churn. It is a place of desperation and longing and roaming ghosts.

All of this is my way of saying that I think it is not empty. This place—an obstacle—is bursting with activity, with microbial adventures, with dancing generativity, with experiments into continuity, with playful meanings and alchemical shifts, with eloquent invocations and stuttered words.

When you meet something fierce, too strong to overcome, too high to climb, too eminent to sidestep, too dark to enlighten, don't take it too personally—you have merely met an antibody, whose sacred task is to challenge you, discombobulate you, disfigure you, and introduce "you" to the strange vastness of your family. A larger commonwealth of becoming.

Just as soils chastise seeds, and cocoons imprison caterpillars, obstacles are the universe's hubs of unspeakable creativity, redeeming us from tired victories, from the banality of crossing the finish line, from the soundtrack of getting everything we want, and especially from the hubris of thinking we are deserving.

•

•

According to some accounts of their history, in precolonial Igboland, the Osu people were revered as a priestly sect dedicated to the service of the gods. They were separate from the people, the freeborn Nwadiala. One did not simply run into them or approach them in a trivial way. To do so might have brought curses on such a person. They were, in fact, untouchable.

Then, one day, Western traders pulled up to our shores. They came with a Bible and a pencil. A weaponized benevolence. Slowly, through the biopower of schooling and the threat of hell, local senses of the sacred began to shift. The altars were left undecorated; no one prayed to Amadioha any longer. No one held onto the breasts of Ala for milk. These fierce winds of change peeled away the veneer of respectability the Osu had as mediators of the divine. In a burnt nutshell, they were no longer untouchable—they had become untouchable.

A queer inflection in meanings. Hidden multiplicities. Emergent significations. The Osu's new "untouchability" was marked by disgust, a notion of uncleanliness and stigma. They were given separate seats in churches, and were not invited to the breaking of the kola. Sons and daughters of the freeborn were not allowed to marry into any family descended from the Osu people. A racialized Soot Black beneath Regular Black on African soil. "Our fathers in their darkness and ignorance called an innocent man Osu," writes Chinua Achebe, "a thing given to idols, and thereafter he became an outcast, and his children, and his children's children forever."[4]

The quantum leap from untouchability to untouchability hints at the universes hidden within the quotidian. The duplicity of the appropriate

---

4 Chinua Achebe writes in his 1960 novel *No Longer at Ease* about the ways the proselytization efforts of Christian missionaries led to self-hatred among Igbo people, and the invention of pathological untouchability among the Osu.

terminology. The mycelial quality of harm that exceeds efforts at "harm reduction."

—

A profoundly respected elder and friend of mine deeply embedded within Peruvian spiritualities and shamanic cosmologies told me a story once: She was leading a party of women and men on a journey. Just as the journey was about to proceed, she insisted that women who were experiencing their periods should wait behind and not proceed with the excursion—given the intensity of the powers at work. Something blew wide open in that cohort; some of the participants were inflamed and offended by this instruction. "How dare you?" they cried. To them, it was a re-imposition of Western-styled exclusionary patriarchal dynamics. They called her names. She attempted to guide their thoughts to something more potent: the consideration that their protests, while legitimate, were nested within layers and sediments of social productions that occluded the hidden meanings of their so-called "exclusion." For this elder friend of mine, this "exclusion" was anything but a modern denial of rights and privileges. Like the way the Ojibwe people perform sacred seclusion rites when a young girl comes of age (rites that connect the motioning and tides of the moon to the murmurations of blood and bodies), or the way some cultures in Nigeria have grandmothers and mothers and aunts "beat up" a young mother who has just put to bed, that is, given birth—dipping her body in hot water and landing maternal blows on her in a painful massage (a practice that has been correlated with the low incidences of postpartum depression among these Nigerians, and which would probably be denounced as "evil" by the West)—this practice of "exclusion" that my friend tried to co-enact was an eco-metaphysical affirmation of great power-with-the-world, a sitting with the sites of tension and rupture, not a denial. Those women were—in the eyes of that moment and of my friend—untouchable. But their politics told them otherwise: that their specific experience exceeded (or rather, came before/preceded) the conditions of its possibility, and that as such to be excluded meant they were, well, untouchable.

—

In my ongoing engagements with the so-called "West," with a certain strand of the English language, with a politics embedded within identitarian categories, and lingering codes of the colonial-universal lurking behind a kind progressive face, I have often had to navigate similar tensions with language, with sayability, with notions of identity and power so foreign to my Western audiences that it seemed the very thought of articulating them would make me implode! Born in a hybrid land of schizophrenic middles, I have known these tensions for a long time. For instance, my schooling taught me that power was tied to voice and how loudly one spoke or how effectively one was represented. But the subtle rhythms of my still-resilient cultural knowledges taught me otherwise: that those who spoke the loudest served the silent (the king does not scream in the marketplace: that is the work of the town crier). These subterranean insights taught me that if one wanted to know power, one had to go to the dark and dense places, not the light places. And that thinking of voice as a container of power—and therefore seeking volume as an expression of that power—was already anchored to a politics of the isolated self that believes voice to be a property of "individuals," instead of an intensity nested within wider fields of mattering.

In the modern West, I continue to with-ness a longing for a politics of emancipation, a beautiful intentionality that is nonetheless an extension of Enlightenment politics—a curious doubling-down on the parameters of the "Human." This "doubling-down" often shows up in the expectation that emancipation is convenient, that some kind of additive politics can be adopted—allowing its constituents to continue along more or less familiar lines of speaking and acting. Nothing too disruptive. For example, the Euro-American machine of climate accountability is still premised on the need to push back against nature-gone-wild, so that even when colorful mottos like "We Are Nature" are deployed by environmentally conscientious actors, the "real" practice unfolds as a centering of the security of human agents within built environments. What that apparatus of response-ability has birthed is a greenwashed economy, which fosters dopaminergic pathways of feeling that tell people in the industrial West they are good people if they recycle their trash—if they keep doing what they do, and if they never give up. What it doesn't tell them is that only 7–10 percent of materials trashed are recycled, and that most of these waste products end up in the refuse bin of progress: the Global South, the great subsidizer of Western righteousness. To most of us who look with curiosity upon the contemporary politics of the West, it often feels like installing solar panels on slave ships.

—

I am convinced that just as a knot on a thread cannot unravel itself except by the disruptive interruption of something outside of it, the colonial enterprise of the "Human" and its many politics of accountability will mostly circle around itself—trapped in its own circularity, in its fixations with categories, in its anxieties about stepping over boundaries, in its shrivelling of abundance to the borders of a pixel ... all done in the holy name of justice. Ironically, I am also convinced that "being offended" is a way out—well, not by itself or in itself, but in the way being offended potentially disturbs the comfort of both the offended and the offender. If nothing disturbs the continuity of the modern and its citizens, it will continue to accommodate itself (in the words of Fred Moten) "violently (and sometimes amelioratively) [within its] quotidian" worlds.[5] Of course, there is something dangerous about presuming that Indigenous people have all the answers and therefore any form of difficulty that comes with processing (or translating) messages is merely the fault of Western thinkers. I refuse that. I don't have answers. We must critique and be critiqued. It is beautiful to be crossed out—that is what it means to be alive in a universe that is hostile to straight lines. I struggle with asking the right questions. None of us can claim answers—not even the gods. Additionally, the category or character of

5 Fred Moten, *In The Break: The Aesthetics of the Black Radical Tradition* (University of Minnesota Press, 2003), 1.

the indigenous is not static or essential, but is also caught up and emergent and seeking.

What is principal to note here then is that when a people gets stuck, when a people gives language too much power, when harm reduction becomes the within-paradigm approach for framing a politics of care, the world in its unspeakable generosities often makes it possible for that stuckness to be haunted and broken open by the shadows of the otherwise. Yes, the Yoruba priest and priestess know menstruation as a "wound"—it is their festive way of celebrating the sickness of being whole; it is why power is nested in mothers, in "Awon Iya Wa"—a power so potent that only those who bleed and those they appoint can come close to "it"; it is their cosmology that thrives upon wounds—not wound-as-pathology (a strange Western inflection) but wound-as-unspeakable-creative-force-for-doing-beauty, wound-as-godflesh—and yes, wound-as-power-to-cause-great-damage to an enemy. And these my mothers would probably celebrate if someone got offended by that! They'd call Esu to dance in the opening.

The Global North needs the South—not because we have answers, but because we have different problems, different ways of speaking, and different ways of being in the world that trouble the monolithicity of the modern. We need each other. It is the only way we might thrive within worlds that know the untouchable are also—untouchable.

•

•

Place is a relationship between bodies that constitutes those bodies, not a static container that merely holds presence. To be in a place is to keep making maps to locate oneself there again and again, and being at home is always an exercise in cartography. So how do we find ourselves in modernity? We keep lists, we name things, we lose them, we filter out information, we adopt positions, we promise, we renege, we try out things. These exercises make "place" an ongoing socio-material dynamic. This suggests that to be displaced is not so much to be chased away from one's land (indeed, displacement can happen without being chased away), as it is to be interrupted by the imposition of a finished product, a complete map. This is the stuff of the colonial: the denial of place and the insertion of the frozen. The toxic gift of arrival.

•

•

When is the imperative to take in the "full picture" an obstacle to transformative differences? We often privilege "big picture" analyses, systemic appraisals, macroeconomic perspectives, and knowledge production values that urge us towards getting all the data and then making a decision. There's something geometrically striking about this urge towards completion or saturation: it risks positioning us, the knowers, outside the analysis, external to the "system." It breeds a forward-facing epistemology of big manifestos and big actors and big dreams of systemic upheavals.

I don't think the world turns exclusively on these industrial notions of change. I think capitalism wants us to "change the world," but it first offers an image that is malleable to its agencies of reinforcement and production. These days, I am learning with my son, who is neuroatypical, about what I joyfully name the animism of peripheral vision, the idea of seeing from the edges, or "looking away at." A refusal to return the gaze of the citizen with one's gaze, a fatal disruption of the interface of sane communication.

There's something about "looking away at" the world that refuses the big picture. Instead it focuses on the ordinary, a crack, a thing, a pixel, a point in spacetime instead of the vaunted entirety of reality that shows up in our theorizations about the world. This dis/ability of "looking away at" is an invitation to lose our way, to not be so invested in the thing's image, to come sensuously alive to other sensorial ethnographies.

Maybe the world changes in small moments. Especially when we are not looking.

•

•

Recently, I gave my son Kyah a wooden jigsaw puzzle toy called Coogam Wooden Blocks. It was a small tablet-sized board composed of delightful, colorful Tetris-shaped pieces. Kyah, my autistic six-year-old prophet of the crossroads, grabbed the thing, unwrapped its plastic wrapping in one fell swoop, and got down to putting the pieces back together.

I wasn't too invested in what he did with the puzzle: I simply wanted him to play, to enjoy himself. Or so I thought. Because when he came back to me moments later with a strange request, I found the low rumbling sound of guttural resistance quite disappointing. Kyah's outstretched hand held one lonely, blue, L-shaped piece of the puzzle. His eyes were keen and focused: "Can you get rid of this for me?"

I explained to him that this wasn't how puzzles worked: "You cannot just toss out a piece if it doesn't fit." He was however adamant, and suggested I throw the piece away. I feigned compliance, slipped the despairing orphan into my pocket, and made a mental note of my invisibly persistent fixation with "usual" outcomes for his play.

Hours later, he returned with more roadkill. "Can you also throw these ones away, please Dada?" In his little hand, he held three of those poor worker pieces, now captive to his whims. He was like a drunk surgeon at an operating table tossing away vital organs that he didn't like. At some level, I recognized that my argument didn't hold much power with him, and yet I tried again to "reason" with him, to urge him to try to work with what he had. To try to complete the puzzle. As I spoke to him, I moved to the table where he had been playing.

And then I saw it.

Kyah had been arranging the pieces according to their commonalities, their shared features, not according to how they had been pre-cut to "complete" the game. He had convened blue rows of L-shaped pieces, black rows of |-shaped pieces, and orange rows of]-shaped pieces. The flat board was now a village of little, spritely shapes in conversation with their kin, stacked upon other princely rows of pieces. Between their parliamentary conversations, awkward and unanticipated gaps emerged—within which nothing could fit. I finally understood why he wanted me to throw away the other wooden pieces: Kyah didn't care about the "big picture," and couldn't care any less about finishing the puzzle. For me, there was only one way to finish it, only one way the makers of the puzzle expected users to play with the pieces; but Kyah—he had found several ways to play that had no neurotypical finish lines.

In the smiling minutes that followed, I realized that while Kyah "had" autism, I "had" oughtism. Oughtism is my name for the ways we are trained, habituated, conditioned, and rewarded to think along dominant lines of production. How we "ought" to behave. A tendency towards the already known. A regulatory refrain that whispers how bodies ought to look, ought to behave. Oughtism is neurotypicality in its production of embodied relations of normo-pathological repetition; it is the sweeping regime of the obvious, a vocation of lines and their secretions, a rush to solutions.

But the obvious can render the world invisible. Kyah's blindness to the obvious is how he strays away from being fully disclosed, being found. Kyah teaches me to look again. Not just at myself but at the world that has never been fully made or rendered. And what's prophecy if not the invitation to look again?

•

•

Prophecy is not a stable prediction of the yet-to-come within an economy of linear temporalities, but the ecstatic intensity of a field of action in which the future and the past are reconvened in a new way. Prophecy is the invitation to not be so sure about where we placed things the last time, the suggestion that nothing is so permanently still that "it" cannot travel. It is the work of commoning in cracks; it is research-with-the-crack. Prophecy is allowing the image to drift away from its fixed coordinates, and making moves to trace the lines of this spillage.

The prophet is not the bearded human figure dramatically poised at the end of history; rather, I would prefer to say that the prophet is the unmaking of time.

•

•

It may just be that the subterranean places we, the fugitives of the present order, must now run to will not be dug out by the hard excavatory machinery of adult logic or the noble spiritualities that claim to know the way but by the gentle seeking fingers of our children caressing the soil, tickling the ground until it guffaws wide open.

•

•

I have been thinking about wounds as striation marks and fault lines that invisibly compose bodies prior to the event of injury. That is, wounds don't come after the fact: the surface might appear smooth, the membrane unpunctured and unperturbed, the skin at rest, but what wholeness occludes is the necessary tensions and troubling experiments in brokenness that keep things alive. We are indebted to this lack of coherence, to this playful gesturing that resists finality. In other words, we are never-not-broken—like the South Asian goddess Akhilandeshwari, whose name is an ode to brokenness. To be embodied is to be in flight. To be embodied is to be beside oneself, perpetually spilling away from resolution.

The modern tendency seems to be to begin our appraisal of bodies from the starting point of "wholeness." Any deviation from this image of normalcy is addressed as something to be fixed, with the prospects of full restoration held as a desirable outcome. But what if we began our stories about how our bodies come to matter—not from the hard portrait of completion, but from the softness of movement? What if we are—like a murmuration of dunlins—a "drunken wounding" dancing with the sky? What if we are echoes of a great blast of life, shockwaves with no original explosion, drifting with spacetime in utter defiance of the modern myths of arrival? And what if what we mean by repair is less restitution to a lost original than a pairing-with-another-composite-body, a re-pair-ing, a borrowing of limbs and organs and tendons from the others around us in order to navigate the complexities of living and dying?

Perhaps nothing captures this ferocious reimagining of bodies as eddies of dust "counterfeiting immobility" like the Japanese art of *kintsugi*, an ancient technique that uses lacquer and gold powder to restore broken ceramics and porcelain vessels. I love the art form, mostly because it implicitly refuses to think of repair as restoration to an original image—and it does this by taking pains to acknowledge the presence of the interface, the decorated crack that marks the irretrievably altered vessel. To think about this art as mere restoration is to elide the agency and contributions of the lacquer, the new glial material that marks the once-quantum potencies and embryonic lines living beneath visibility. The first time I observed a kintsugi-repaired piece, I said to myself: "It's still broken; the artist has just mapped this rich encounter of loss, memory, and longing with gold." Kintsugi is the art that reminds us that everything is already broken.

To be re-paired is to be re-coupled-with-an/other in an ever-moving, carnivalesque, and alien cavalcade of exchangeable organs and reiterable subjectivities. The monster is not the brutal beast standing in the way of our imperial march of imperviousness; the monster is the irresistible reminder of our molecular debt to this multispecies "migritude"[6] of all things.

•

6 Shailja Patel coins the term "migritude" in her memoir of the same name (*Migritude*, 2010), performing the concept as a rich tapestry, in Jennifer Leetsch's words, of "strategies of addressing, negotiating, and ultimately opposing [white-supremacist] violence that all play out along differing visual, textual, and material routes." It is Patel's resistance of modern tropes of belonging that reduce it to spatiotemporal uniformity. Jennifer Leetsch, "Playing with Saris: Material and Affective Unfoldings of Violence and Resistance in Shailja Patel's *Migritude*," *Interventions* 23, no. 5 (2021): 691–711, accessed March 2024, https://doi.org/10.1080/1369801X.2021.1885469.

•

Brokenness is not secondary to wholeness. Not the means to an end. Not a thing apart, complete and all by itself. In the same way, darkness is not merely the absence of light. There are imperatives woven into the thick that illumination knows nothing about. There are wisdoms only cracks can articulate. There are tunes only accessible to low frequencies. There are pathways that stretch out fabulously only in the stoic obstruction of an impediment. Perhaps music is the rushing air forced out from the shrinking space between a boot and a neck. Perhaps there is life ... even here, there is life.

•

•

"Speak truth to power!"
"Raise your voice to be heard."
"Let voices speak for themselves."

Perhaps nothing else carries as much weight in contemporary activism and qualitative inquiry as the "voice." Voice is what we throw at the offending powers; voice is what we insist on exercising in the face of exclusion; voice is the highway to transcendence, the vehicle that conveys the inviolable truth of authentic inner experience and represents our rights to a good life. Voice is data. The thing to do then is to create spaces for a polyvocal politics where multiple voices can be heard, where the singular is upset by the many.

The problem with this reductive conception of voice is that, among other troubling assumptions, voice seems to be the outworking of an ideological commitment to the anthropocentric individual—the humanist subject who owns voice and experience. By thinking of voice as propertied, as something I own, as an independent weapon to wield in a field of contesting voices, we inadvertently preserve the myth of the stable speaker.

From the perspective of the Afrocene, we are neither the owners of "our" voices nor the valedictorians of "our" experiences. There is no stable speaker, no secure "voicer" behind the voice. When we speak, we might very well be effects of an ecological ventriloquism that enlists bodies—even in a politics defined by antagonistic sides—to the reproduction of its materialities. In this sense, speaking truth to power becomes a way for power to reassert itself.

This does not mean we get rid of voice. We will often need to speak out, to pin our ninety-five theses on the wooden doors of the establishment. However, there's something about resituating voice within an animist milieu—especially as a strategic move in these times of sticky paradoxes—that permits us to explore not just the limits of vocality but the generativity of fugitive "silence." The irreducible transcorporeality in never fully owning one's experiences.

•

•

Mispronunciations are post-human phenomena: they are reminders that language is not even ours to master or control. Language is not the thing that comes from our mouths, but an undulating terroir of speakability and non-speakability—often rising to the zenith-like clarity of grammar and syntax, but never quite removing itself completely from the lowlands of simmering silences, limbic gestures, and occultic shadows.

In other words, we speak like the environments we live in, because those environments are neither external nor distant matters. We speak like the foods we eat, like the excretions of bacteria in our guts, like the technologies and algorithms that summon us, and like the textures that greet us day to day. We speak only within ecologies that matter. For that reason, to speak is to be limited. To speak is to be indebted to animal, ancestral, microbial oddkin.[7]

Growing up in Lagos, Nigeria, this—of course—was not the understanding of language my childhood teachers worked with. I remember being forced to pronounce English names and words correctly—for grades and prizes.

There was always this white BBC presenter on the old screen, whose proper pronunciations were allowed to be the standard for our own local English accents. I ran into a lot of problems pronouncing the schwa sound while trying to stop myself from laughing. But my teachers were serious: the word wasn't "fatha," it was "fath-er." "When in Rome, you must behave like the Romans," they would say, as if to justify the curriculum of capture they were also shackled to. The problem with saying

---

7 Donna Haraway's playful deployment of the term "oddkin" in her book *Staying with the Trouble* celebrates the many other ways kinship might be formulated beyond blood relations. See: Donna J. Haraway, *Staying with the Trouble: Making Kin in the Chthulucene* (Duke University Press, 2016).

things like that was that I wasn't in "Rome"; well, not quite. I didn't ask for "Rome." Rome came to us, uninvited.

While I understand ongoing concerns about the ways dominant groups treat the material treasures of minoritarian peoples and Indigenous cultures—for there are moments, not without risks, when we need walls that seal off things—I am myself often delighted when my name is mispronounced.

I recall a particular time when, as we got ready to record our conversation, my interviewer asked for clarity on how to properly say my last name. She wouldn't even attempt a pronunciation; she didn't want to mess it up. Laughing, I urged her to "give it a shot," to make an effort. She insisted I pronounce it first, waiting for me to give in to her anxieties. I didn't. I dug in, and encouraged her to try. Pursing her lips, her eyes dropping for a second in resignation, she articulated it: "Ah-ko-mo-laf?" It sounded vaguely Russian, so I celebrated the moment, and then addressed her confusion:

"The Yoruba people don't mind when others mispronounce their names. We celebrate the gift of mispronunciation: it affords us new opportunities to meet ourselves again as if for the first time. To hear the multiplicity and comical indeterminacy that haunts recognition.

"If everyone got it right on the first try, what an awful cosmology that would be. It is because my name is not fully mine that I can trust you to bend it, twist it, and risk making it something else altogether. But if I do not risk your mispronunciation, I also foreclose the opportunity to become different, to taste new things. Your limitations are also my name."

Yes. Our names are sacred because they are never complete in themselves. They are not inert "things" that "belong" to us. They are migrant stories that do things on their own. May our names travel and play, learn and bless. May we be response-able parents to them. May they get lost enough to encounter new realities, and may they return to us often, bright-eyed and muddy, to tell us of things we never could consider had they not brought home new friends they picked up along the way.

•

•

The liberal world order, anchored in humanist presuppositions, spins and turns on the majesty and exclusivity of the human individual.

This individual is fully realized: he has intentions; he has rationality; he has language; he has agency; and he can solve problems. Nothing escapes him. The world begins and ends at the boundaries of his will. The entire enterprise of progress and the prospects for peace are premised on this rational individual exercising his divine rights to forge a world for himself. A world deserving of his appearing.

But the crises streaming through the post-Hiroshima world of ticking clocks, purring machines, and universal declarations are transversal guests. They do not bow at the imperial figure of the Man. These troubles are entrained with this world, but cannot be fully reduced to it. They are this-worldly and otherworldly all at once. They are prophetic in that they render visible the outlines by which our lives are contained and textured.

In the blast of their rapturous crossing, we are compelled to consider a "bigger" force than the Man. We are forced to notice the vigorous potency of archetypal flows; the near-primordial humming of cavernous entities lurking beneath the humdrum of the modern; the mythopoeic excursions of the orishas; the molecular experiments of the subatomic; the espionage of bacteria; the lamentations of ancestral ghosts.

In the wake of their passing, rumors are that the world does not in fact turn on what we do, what humans do. That we are not alone and never were. That being kind and compassionate, eloquent and smart, this and that, is not enough. That achieving a sense of "inner" balance, organizational success, or moral purity might actually prove ironically stultifying to the strange business of becoming-otherwise. In short, the liberal futures predicated on humans getting their act together are defunct, forever postponed, useful perhaps only as framed portraits dotting the hallways dedicated to the myth of our sovereignty.

This is why it is impossible to think about the challenges we face today squarely in terms of human actions and human projects. A posthumanist, animist inflection reminds us that problems are how moral-aesthetic-epistemo-ontological arrangements (otherwise, "natures") become creative, and solutions are how those very arrangements often fortify themselves.

We'd need more than getting our acts together to address the crippling challenges of our time. Indeed, we might need to come apart.

•

•

What if rationality—that singular virtue Enlightenment philosophers and poets extolled as the quintessential trait of the Human—was but the secretions of microbial parasites long paired with "human" bodies?

What if our loftiest achievements owed their buoyancy to the actions of little germs wriggling in the darkness of their prosthetic externality, stirring the cauldrons of their own experiments with life and becoming?

What if we've never been human?

•

•

This is what it means to be entangled: it is to see that we are not complete, removed, or boundaried. We are not independent. To speak from a place of manicured morality, to attempt to stand outside the mess of it all, to try to be sincere, is to be blind to our rapturous entanglement with the multiple. A "flower" doesn't "begin" at its roots and terminate abruptly at its petals; it is the ongoing intra-activity (notice I do not say "interactivity," for this would suggest that "things" preexist relationships) of clouds, rain, sunlight, swirling dust, the keen attention of the gardener, and a cocktail of colorful critters and ecosystems of organisms. One might say that there are no "things" at all. To come to the edge is thus to come to the curdling middle, where wild meets wild, where we "meet the universe halfway"[8] in acknowledgment of our intra-dependence and co-emergence with "movements" we cannot control or assuage.

Perhaps in situating his home at the edge of the village, the healer reminds himself and everyone else that we are not the central concern of an unspeakable universe. We are reminded of the ineffable, that words are not little epistemological mirrors that can reflect the state of things. We are part of the world's ongoing complexity, yes, but not its prime movers, sole actors, or longed-for apotheoses. As such, all the qualities we think of as unique to humans—thought, agency, will, intentionality, creativity, subjectivity—are performative qualities of a larger field in constant flux. Thus in order to really account for ourselves, in order to tell the stories of what is happening, we must come to the ends of ourselves, we must gravitate towards the edges in the middle ... towards the incomprehensible, where wholly new ways of thinking are gestating in puddles of the forgotten.

•

---

8 Karen Barad, *Meeting the Universe Halfway: Quantum Physics and the Entanglement of Matter and Meaning* (Duke University Press, 2007).

•

Here's a riddle: What is more powerful than power?

In my initial explorations of Indigenous Yoruba cosmo-vision stories, I encountered an epic saga of strange arrivals, complicit kings, broken gods, and their struggles with European colonialism.

In one particular story about the orishas and their response to the activities of the long-drawn-out Middle Passage, a tale that springs from the wealth of our speculative fabulations, Ogun—the god of iron, metal, truth, and justice—prepares to battle the newly arrived slave traders. To definitively defeat them and send them packing. In divine fury, he rushes to the beach to assert his power, but is intercepted by Esu—his trickster brother, the "man of the crossroads"—who cajoles him into lying down and drinking some palm wine. Ogun succumbs to the wily Esu, and sleeps away his D-Day. Meanwhile, Esu steals into the ship's hold, and travels across the Atlantic Ocean to creolize the world.

At first blush, this account of things might be disconcerting to many who equate power with agency. You might ask, why would Esu allegedly enable the slave traders in their abhorrent vocation of capturing bodies and wounding generations? What is the gift of thinking with this strange story?

The riddle I have offered above, indebted to this story, reframes the narrative of loss and decimation without dismissing these tragedies. It troubles history, disturbs the archive, challenges the power of the historian, and strays from a humanist notion of power as "agency," or power as mastery.

When the Yoruba trickster Esu traveled with the slave ships across the waters to the "New World," he perturbed the colonial project, inscribing it with a tense duplicity that rendered the Middle Passage in new ways. By infusing those carceral vessels with his energies, he corrupted the master's categorical objectives of domination. He untied the strings that bound control to power and hid himself in the bloodied wounds of the "powerless." What might have been a business operation to capture bodies for the industrial desires of the plantation, a floating jail cell for the captured, became the engorged womb of worlds-to-come. The hull of the slave ship was now pregnant with black joy, the merrymaking rhythms of samba, the tastes and delicacies of creolized futures. The ship was no longer just "this" or "that"; it was crackling with strange life.

From a postactivist perspective, the view that power is simply "the capacity to do things" obscures the singular risk of being powerful: entrapment. This is the trick that haunts mastery: to gain lordship over someone is to be in touch-with; it is to cede just as much ground as one might need to control/enslave/own others. To become a master over the "other" is to touch the other, and thus open up pathways of being undone from within. The wound cuts both ways.

As the intensity of a particular configuration of bodies in relation to each other, power can be a jail cell, an inversion of the senses, a blindness to myriad intelligences, a Faustian deal. Instead of being a stable property, it is a field of practices, a way of naming ourselves, a way of participating-with. Power can keep us bound to certain ways of speaking, knowing, thinking, and relating.

As such, to contest power and achieve victory might seem desirable on the surface, but we risk being eaten up by the field of practices that are the conditions of our suffering.

Esu, prince of duplicity, seems to understand this. Instead of declaring war, he guides the ships to the shores; he infiltrates the contact zone, the place where mastery plants its flag; he flows into the hold; he lives inside a rag doll; he murmurs through the moaning of the captured; among the captors on the upper deck, he laughs the hardest when they force their prisoners to dance for the amusement of the captain; his mockery transmutes into a suggestion that blossoms in the imaginations of the discarded: entertainment provides cover for novelty of a seditious kind. The seed of a martial art, a queer form of resistance. The first flicker of capoeira.

What is more powerful than power?

•

•

If the Anthropocene is the broken slave ship and its rituals of restoration, the Afrocene is the simmering, dimly illuminated, watery distance in the crack of the hull—a sensuous whisper, a goddess beckoning, a third path between the anorexic binary of accountability versus apathy. The gravity of things pulling the whole contraption down into depths. Into excess. The disruptive, anarranging shock to forward movement. An invitation to get lost. To become-fish. To become-water.

•

•

The structure that allocates identity and fixes it in place also befogs the ongoingness of these "identities," blinding the eye from noticing how spread out we are, how the many colors we take on bend with the play and openings and closures of topographical shifts, climatic changes, and biological matterings.

To speak of Blackness as if it were an essence or Whiteness as if it were a "fixed other," a final evil to be conquered, is to ironically extend the reach of white normativity. Race is more-than-human; it is apophatic, resisting complete analysis; a flowing coproduction of bodies in troubling fidelities, prosthetic arrangements, and relationships.

Black bodies are not the products of Black ancestries traced "back," merely burdened with inheritance; embodiment is more complex than articulated lineages. Instead, Black bodies are the intra-acting negotiation of bodies, climate, economic power, theological categories, and the modern will to power, purpose, and direction. A certain horizontality is missing from a politics that always begins its thesis from the positionality of the finished individual—and is therefore always already too late.

For Blackness to be generative beyond the gridlock of modern subject, we need to reimmerse it within quantum flow. We would need a way of talking about our bodies as if they were constantly spirited away—because they are.

•

•

I refuse to speak in the language of totalizing absolutes, pure arrivals, or complete archives, whether in reference to the "villains" of contemporary countercultural politics (capitalism, humanism, colonialism, and yes even racism), or to the anticipated good their total banishment would purportedly impose. This is because the ways we attempt to respond to these "villains" often entangle us within their sticky ontologies.

Our "anti-this"/"anti-that" postures and treasured analyses of the shortcomings of dominant power (which are indeed quite necessary to minoritarian projects of survival within oppressive systems) are also risky dances with colonial capture. I know this from the perpetual incarceration of African nation-states even after more than a hundred years of successful African struggles for independence from colonial powers; I know this from the received legends of swashbuckling heroes becoming the enemies they supposedly vanquished; I understand this from the warnings of Indigenous elders about the risks of being seen and the traps of getting what we want, and from feminist insights that point to the somatic effervescence and volatility of bodies which disturb stable boundaries and convenient plots.

When Nigerian philosopher-singer Aṣa croons in her song "Jailer," "I'm a prisoner / you're a prisoner too, Mr. Jailer," she means to say that there are forces of entrapment and manumission at work that exceed the grunge immediacy of shackles and the pleasure of wielding the whip. She (at least the version of her in my head!) means to point us to the forces of convergence that bind our freedom movements to the same colonial epistemological arrangements that grant our bodies and futures coherence.

Perhaps what we need alongside our more recognizable modes of engagement are new patterns of analysis that tune us to the migrancy of things—to molecular spillages and not just identity categories; to a metaphysics of im/possibilities and not just a metaphysics of presence; to haunting absences; to what white bodies are becoming and to how even white bodies (and the world-building/world-naming ritual that we often name as "whiteness") are caught up within desirous forces of errancy, loss, and failure. When we essentialize white bodies as faits accomplis, pure expressions of villainy, instead of creaturely becomings no less fugitive than minoritarian bodies, we inadvertently participate in (and risk reinforcing) a cosmology of fixed things, fixed bodies, closed identities, and Euclidean geometries.

Decoloniality is the undecidability of things, of positions, of objects, of concepts, of bodies. It is the poetic appraisal that invites us to be hesitant in our naming things, to be wary of trophies, to be quick on our feet.

If our visions of the horizon aren't changing, then it means we're standing still.

•

•

Stuckness is the effect of sameness. Homogenization. Alienation. It is when the manifold relations, practices, gestures, intensities, thresholds, exclusions, tensions, imaginations, and body-subjectivities—summoned and partially articulated or territorialized by morality—have an effect of convergence, reproducing troubling dynamics, orientations, and sensorial imperatives.

It is when the critique and the critiqued both feed each other and are sustained by a mutual indigestibility that stabilizes the "other" in perpetuity.

It is when climate action ignites a field of practice whose circuitry retraces the outlines of an anthropocentric imperviousness to impermanence, to demise, to the vibrant animacies of a world not entirely available for our comfort or survival.

It is when an identity politics arises in response to painful colonial infractions by insisting on a seat at the table of power constructed with technologies of dissociation.

It is the torturous cyclicity of a shackled Prometheus facing the wrath of Zeus, his divine liver healing spontaneously only to be eaten again and again by the terrifying eagle that prompted the regeneration in the first place.

Stuckness is when healing produces bodies that are resources for surveillance and subjectivization.

But perhaps the most evocative figure of stuckness is the eon-long war between Popeye and Bluto, the devas and asuras, the left and the right, good and evil, and the binaries that populate our politics.

When things get stuck, the morality that sponsors the constituents of this carceral dynamic has come to the limits of its worldmaking rituals, and itself yearns to travel. This is why the trickster travels. This is why the trickster refuses to heal displacements. This is how the world moves.

•

•

From a processual, non-representational, post-humanist perspective, every social encounter paraphrases bodies in the sweltering heat of intra-action. Indeed, one cannot meet another without becoming modified. "Our" identities—never reducible to choice or preference—do not predate the relational arrangements that are the condition of their emergence. Failure is the very ground of encounter.

In some sense then, we drunkenly tumble through a hall of distorting mirrors wherein every surface that greets us is a risk, bending, stretching, pulling, rethreading the inauthentic, cavorting with unseen possibilities. Even "normal" mirrors have hidden careers. We will not be seen. We will not be heard. We will not be reproduced. We will be paraphrased.

The morality that situates itself on exact reproductions, on the sociality of proper pronunciations, on the articulation of violent harm as premised on a failure to communicate, on the expectation that one's identity is exclusively a chosen or preferred referent that every meaningful encounter must honor, will most likely produce a society of bodies impervious to each other, radically inhospitable to the undercurrents of life in the lowercase—and is itself a product of such an arrangement: a secretion of a brutal humanism that seeks to extract the finished product of safety, the finished product of prior coherence, a finished image of authenticity from the labor of a thousand cuts in the hopes that in reproducing a still image we might postpone the debt we owe to the fading away that loves all things.

•

•

If colonization placed us in boxes, one might think that "decolonization" is the act of coming out of the box. Moving from here to there. But that would be another silent instance of imperialism—another capitulation to the mythical condition that enlists us in the practice of seeing things as discrete, not relational; as simple, not complex and partial; as dead, not alive and agential.

The attempt to come "out of the box" would then be a denial that even "the box" is part of nature's doing. It would be a reassertion of our trust that the sacred lies in attaining distance from where we are—and that in the gilded and glistening "there" dwell complete resolutions to the challenges and problems we face "here."

Decolonization is not about moving from "here" to "there"; it is a weirding of the distance between the two. Decolonization is not a category, a property, or a thing in itself—it is a queering of things, of relationships, of assumptions. A stunning "what if?" that pulses in the veins of our necropolis. It is an ethical call flowing with the currents of things, inviting us to listen to the murmurs of the supposedly "dead" and "instrumental" world around us. It is the rift in the spaces of power suggesting that there are many other ways to become-with the world that disturb the hegemony of humans and human interests.

And this brings me back to the point I began with: don't come out of the box; decorate its walls. Touch the box. Embroider its corners. Pour libations on its floors. Press your ears against its textured surfaces. In your awkward alliance, you will learn that enchantment is not in short supply, even in the places that feel most bereft of it. And you yourself will not be left intact.

•

•

There's a deceptively simple yet pervasive expectation that all of us—everyone—could summarily arrive at the right version of things, the true story, outside of the blaringly misleading headlines, outside of misinformation campaigns, outside of unprocessed biases and legacies, outside of the manipulation of giant media and corporate algorithms. And that with a little prodding here and there, a little coaching and educational support (perhaps I underestimate how much prodding and coaching is often anticipated), we can climb out of the rapidly flowing murky and anfractuous river unto the banks of right thinking.

We can think straight—finally!—because we now read the rest of the story and not just the headlines; we can think straight because we now question our sources more frequently instead of jumping to conclusions; we can think straight because we understand our limitations and trust those who have done the research to speak.

The problem of course is that this expectation religiously presumes a rational infrastructure to behavior, a hard steel floor of correct thinking beneath the shifty strata of cloudy half-processed dross. It presumes we, like snakes shedding worn-out skin, can remove ourselves, perhaps with great difficulty, from underneath the sedimentation that has kept us buried in heresy. And that by and by, we can think properly. It presumes we can leave the rapidly flowing muddy river for its sturdier banks. But this river has no banks, and there is no place to stand.

We are the river in its messy frothing flows. We are oriented bodies, swept away, driven, stirred, instigated, swayed, marked, moved and moving, cultured, struck through, diagonal, contradictory, implicated, complicit, political, inchoate, exposed, shifting, migrant, and populated. And the feeling of security granted by presuppositions of rational and positivistic foundations is like a man who has tied himself to flotsam, hoping that the stuff is anchored to something that is "not river." Something more dependable than this sullen tide.

•

•

You may have heard it said that love is a bridge that connects all things. But such a perspective still leaves the world split between two matters: things and bridges. Bodies and connections. If love is in fact a bridge, it is a bridge that cuts deep and pushes so far into the flesh of the thing it seeks to connect to another thing that it becomes indistinguishable from the body.

I think love is a gaping wound in the project of final closure, the postponement of completion, the magic that refuses absolute independence to any one thing and makes bodies like fluid spirits and material becomings. With a bridge, I can turn away from crossing. But love exceeds static notions of agency, enlisting us in its queer mattering and desirous inquiries in ways we cannot fathom or language.

I think love is not a bridge at all: I think love is a hyphen, an umbilical cord, the undoing of the master's sword, the aching at the heart of creation, the vaginal opening that mocks arrivals and departures, the promise that we will never be fully done or done with.

•

•

The troubling Aristotelian presupposition that our bodies are a collection of senses, or that we have the sense of smell, the sense of taste, of sight, of touch, of this and that, quantized senses neatly delineated from the other, is not entirely remediated by insisting we have "more than five senses," or even by blurring the lines between those senses, as in the case of synesthesia.

I don't think bodies "have" senses per se in the way phones "have" apps. Instead, I think bodies are the coagulative gesturing of sensorial flows. That is, bodies are how senses do their work. It is not bodies and their senses, it is senses as embodied materialities of inquiry. In this sense, the blind person isn't merely said to be missing the sense of sight; the blind person is a collective performance of a world that exceeds vision and optical clarity.

Senses are therefore not just dissociated bodily abilities; they are ethical, sociopolitical, technological, economic, affective arrangements that ignite bodies in terrifying and poetic worlding processes. This idea of seeing senses, not as items in a shopping cart, not as neuro-reductive events, but as enlistments of specific kinds, is why deaf and blind poet and teacher John Lee Clark "writes" about the dangers of access and the violence of visuality: "I pity the sighted."

•

•

The promise of transformation is indebted to, and must depend upon, how disability is reframed—not as lack, but as queer abundance.

•

•

Nihilism might be a deeper form of caring than most might appreciate. An abundance of attachment instead of a critical loss of it. On the surface, the nihilist stands apart in his claims that nothing matters. At least, this is how a lot of what passes as nihilism is characterized: nothing matters. From this pathologizing distance, we might view this detached, cold imperviousness with scorn. In the face of so much suffering, how can one not care?

Against the run of things, I would argue that it would require a certain kind of vibrancy, a certain kind of flirtatious aliveness and quavering animacy, a being within the fragile world in some way, an orgasmic touching of things, a falling in love with matter, with the matrixial edge of the world in her fugitive openness, to come to the idea that nothing matters.

I am not merely trying to say that the articulation of nihilism is the expression of the nihilist's frustrations with the world, an indication of a previous capacity to care for the world. That may be so, but I would gesture at something stranger: that the stance of indifference, the seemingly stable point of meaninglessness, is already struck through with a finer tension, a deep caring, a seeking of some kind that wants to fly towards the sun with wax-clad wings instead of staying carefully within the atmosphere of the already known. In this sense, nihilism feels like an excess instead of an absence. What is at stake? Well, nothing matters. Nothing's mattering. Nothing's materiality. Nothing's materiality, speculative buoyancy, and radical hospitality is at stake.

As such, I find it interesting to think of nihilism together with paraontology.[9] Nihilism's interest is in how "nothing" comes to matter because it senses the inadequacies of "everything." Its gravitational pull and intrigue is towards the apophatic, unsayable, para-moral, and negative outsides that lurk at the edges of everything. A para-ontology. "Everything" is not enough. "Nothing" makes sense. The sweltering compost heap of nothing, useless to the violent renderings of everything, harbors the unsaid, the autistic, the unworlding of worlds, the poverty of meaning.

Indeed, I am compelled to think of blackness as necessarily nihilistic. Postactivism is nihilistic. A fugitive nihilism, if you will. The crack has no goal, no end, no utopia in mind.

Maybe this is why I have always been intrigued by nothing and the way it comes to matter: in those moments when my childhood pastor urged me to remember that God had created everything, I would whisper under my breath that everything was too small to encompass my interests.

Nothing also matters.

•

9 Nahum Chandler popularized the term "paraontology." But my reading here thinks with Fred Moten's and Erin Manning's deployment of the term to name a "blackness" that sidles systemic closures, exiling itself from white settlement. See: Nahum Chandler, "Of Exorbitance: The Problem of the Negro as a Problem for Thought," in *X: The Problem of the Negro as a Problem for Thought* (Fordham University Press, 2013); Fred Moten, "The Case of Blackness," *Criticism* 50, no. 2 (2008): 177–218, https://doi.org/10.1353/crt.0.0062; Erin Manning, *The Minor Gesture* (Duke University Press, 2016).

•

Sometimes, what we want looks nothing like what our eyes have been so fervently taken by.

Outside the image, outside the spoils of imagination, outside the anxious traffic of language, an earthworm wriggles into the loam; a lichen yawns its many arms into being; a crow lifts her head; a dragonfly flutters to the east, the rest of the universe tied to her abdomen; and Dostoyevsky's returned and rejected messiah despairingly considers the shackles on his feet.

It is a mistake to suppose that in these times of disquieting tragedies what we want are mere solutions, or that our minds can even encompass, let alone articulate, the breadth and weight of what the world is doing in its own unspeakable wanting.

It might just be that the troubling solutions we celebrate are the tolerable fixes we deploy to soothe the aching of the inexpressible, the impossible, the haunting at the edges of grammar. Sooner than later, we will have to meet new political constituencies, awkward others we could not have imagined, strange familiars that dwell in the worlds outside the image that lovingly imprisons us.

•

•

When a new god is to be born, a crack tears through the flesh of things—through which a meandering signal, a prophecy long-traveled, arrives in our midst. If we accompanied these wander lines, this signal, messenger of a body-not-yet-formed, veins etched with fire and shadow in the troublingly smooth moral horizons, straying away from the vortices of the known and the good, we would never arrive. There is no destination awaiting us. Instead, we would keep walking. And then we would die—and our bodies and bones would be fed to the grounds that fed us in our journeying.

Somehow this becoming-lost, this accompanying the uncomely signal, this pressing of the feet against the soil, this shuffling of bodies through disconcerting winds, this faint gesturing towards a song we yearn to grasp, this eating and being eaten up, would trace out the umbilical cord of the neonate god-to-come. Our bodies, carried in morsels by critters too busy to name, would be the god's organs. Its tissues, membranes, cells, lungs, heart, kidneys, and vocal cords. Its life and unspeakable passing.

•

•

Every winter, with a ready tune, an ancient wind seduces the Bodélé Depression at the edge of the Sahara Desert. The Depression, might I remind you, is the dustiest place on earth, a seven-thousand-year-old graveyard that marks the site of a once great lake that is no more. The wind's seductive tunes launch a grand procession, a planetary ritual, a burial ceremony that will carry the aged elderly shells of long-dead diatoms—single-celled algae with crystalline walls for bodies—across the curdling Atlantic Ocean in lavish plumes of humming and moaning.

Now, if you had Icarian wings and could hold your breath in outer space, you would be able to see this procession of dancing ghosts stretching from the African continent to the Caribbean, alighting on the grateful and verdant Amazonian lungs of this planet. A festival of the dead. The Elder Children of Homeless Wind and Dry Ground. A pilgrimage of bones.

Yes.

The stunning implication of this planetary exercise isn't lost on climate scientists and atmospheric chemists who study this yearly ritual closely: without this migrant sea of precious dust spilling from the shores of Africa, from the dead womb of the carcass of the once mighty Lake Mega Chad, the Amazon—a leaching system characterized by the constancy of heavy rainfall that washes away nutrient-rich soil—cannot supply the planet with oxygen. These silicon coffins play an enormous role in the world's photosynthesis, shaping our lives whether we notice or not. Coming to think about this delicate (and largely invisible) work takes one's breath away: we cannot breathe without the prolific generativity of the dead.

This is the stuff of worship.

•

•

Your life is not the breathing space squeezed between your birth and your demise. In fact it is not your life as such. You own none of it: your failures, your disappointments, your accidents, your successes, your failed attempts at mastery, and your many inabilities.

They are no one's property. They are a sweeping movement of becomings that counterfeit immobility, the cloudy plumes of relations that bring shape and form and color to everything.

You are the denseness of those unspeakably intricate gestures, those bodily signals that connect bare stone and spinning galaxy in a single sigh. We are always of the village, and the thorns in our flesh are gifts of the previous as well as the yet to come.

Reading this, you might hastily conclude that life is about surrendering. And that if life isn't ours to live or own, then there is no sense to being accountable. If our lives weren't ours, wouldn't that absolve us from the kinds of responsibilities that make for practical materialities of care? Wouldn't we be giving up too much to a wishy-washy notion of entanglement that knows nothing of the fierce everydays we contend with?

To that I would say that life is also in the not-surrendering. In the gasping for air. In the muscles' taut resistance to being squelched by the limbs of an assailant. In seeking distance and abstraction. Life-death (for they must be considered as meandering lines of intimacy) is a thresholding, a differentiation, a traveling-with. Perhaps life's abjection and non-legibility might gently coax us to consider that it is not simply the opposite of death; that it is not ours to live per se; that life exceeds conceptualizations of instrumentality, authenticity, purpose, and direction; and that it will not be reduced to a set of convenient principles or ideological formulations.

To displace us from the perch of ownership is not to pull down our sails—it is to notice that the winds offer more than mere direction.

•

•

There seems to be a problem with the assertion that the world is reducible to story; that we humans are the storytellers at the heart of this cosmic saga; and that this generation, burdened with the failures of a civilization that seems outclassed by its own ambitions, must convene a new story to carry us into some new age.

The trouble here is that such an assertion worryingly flattens the cosmos to familiar parameters of intelligibility. To language. To meaning. To accessibility. And, in doing so, by flattening the frame to its pixel, proponents of a story-is-all approach leave out a world that matters in ways that are not always available for scrutiny, for discourse, for thought.

I am reminded of the great boasts of the fabled second king of the Babylonian Empire, Nebuchadnezzar II, who at one time attributed the genius of said empire to his agency. It is said that the gods punished him by driving him insane, causing him to "eat grass as oxen." Nebuchadnezzar lived like a cow for seven years, a boanthropic infliction that marked a divine gesture, an invitation to be suspicious of our stories—or at least to notice that the world does not orbit around human agency alone. Indeed, if we take for granted the famous aphorism that suggests the gods make mad those whom they love the most, we might intuit that the universe is transversally composed in part by insanity, by the unspeakable, by the shocking, mouth-stopping passing of a wild god in a firmament of black silence.

By investing too heavily in the promises of language and narrative, we reinforce a logocentric universe that conveniently situates us in the center of all things. Much to our chagrin and penury. Moreover, giving story too much power blinds us to the actions of the world around us, and to the ways we too are convened, adopted, oriented, moved, appellated, enlisted, and governed by things without name and plot. These queer absences and ghostly gaps haunt the totalizing containment of story, pulling it down to earth from its gilded perch in the heavens.

I like to think that the night sky, pregnant with stars and wonders, through the eons of its hypnotic dance, has struck down many a traveler, many a songstress, many a griot. Like it struck down Nebuchadnezzar of old. We too need this medicine, this striking down that brings about errancy and play. Perhaps something about the capacity of the world to stand in our way, to disrupt the impervious path, to sully the journey with its filth, makes room for the sacred. For awe. For reverence. For a becoming-animal. For a thick silence that knows that it too is known, that it too is reshaped in its efforts to shape the world.

We will not unilaterally story a new world into being. The world is not just story, it is silence. The world is not just system, it is glitch. The world is not just presence, it is absence. The world is not world, it is unheard of.

•

•

Grief is nomadological.[10] That is to say, it is concerned with nomads and the settlements they traverse. Here, the nomad is loss. One might then say that grief is the itinerancy of loss; it is how loss travels; how it infiltrates structures, decays edges, and forces new postures of reverence and irreverence. Grief is how loss traverses the dominant tendencies of the city, upsetting continuity, undoing identity, exposing edges.

Of course, the American Psychological Association might disagree with this reading of grief as an impersonal, potentially decolonizing force—or maybe they do agree, implicitly, because their nosological descriptions of grief tell us that one year is enough time to experience grief over loss. After this duration, grief is pathological, because it would then get in the way of one's life. In this sense, our sociopolitical systems are increasingly defined by a struggle to make grief a good citizen, to make it productive towards pre-constituted tendencies of world production. The quest to contain the outbreak of grief is how white stability reasserts itself.

This is why I am keenly interested in the virology of grief, in the animism of grief—in those moments it can no longer be contained and processed and archived and locked away. It is in those moments of spillage, moments of lamentation, when sobs become yelps, when yelps become lycanthropic howls, when howls drive us to the dust, when we lose the dignity of outward presentability and our bodies are contorted into new shapes, that we become immersed in new feedback loops, ancient patterns of sensing, and new choreographies of possibility.

Lamentation is grief emancipated from its productivity.

•

10 Gilles Deleuze and Félix Guattari, *Nomadology: The War Machine*, trans. Brian Massumi (Semiotext(e), 1986).

•

"Bacchanal aesthetics."

That was what Trinidadian novelist Earl Lovelace called "it"—the contemporary invitation to appropriate the cultural practices of New World slaves as they responded to oppression beneath the metal boot of imperial forces.

But why would Lovelace use a word like "bacchanal" (from Bacchus, the Roman god of wine and pleasure; used to indicate wild and drunken orgiastic celebrations) to describe the ethical responses of captives to the mechanisms of their incarceration? Why associate the archetypal figure of parties with the tragedy of slavery?

In a sense, the bacchanal was the wild outgrowth of a strange sort of resistance—one that did not thrive exclusively on pitchforks and revolutions, but found abundance in the hidden, in the subterranean, in subterfuge, in seeking the riven places of the gilded interiority of the plantation. The bacchanal said: when you are outnumbered, do fractions: explore the weakness of power, seek ecstasy, touch the duplicity of your jail cell, bury your rituals and longings for home in the vacuous cadavers of your master's gods, hide the seditious sounds of samba beneath the cacophony of cooking so that the authorities do not understand the deep intelligences at work.

The bacchanal is the wild intensity of a crack, the generativity of disability that the glistening surfaces of the capable cannot handle. The Dionysian depths are only accessed by the pressure of displacement and loss, by the dis/human. Lovelace's "bacchanal aesthetics" displaces power as central to the workings of the world. The point is not to overcome power with power, but to disappoint power's claims to totality (an idea that Afro-Martinican philosopher Édouard Glissant called "the right to opacity").[11] "Bacchanal aesthetics" is a call to cultivate a different politics of being response-able to the necropolitics[12] of the master. Far from being an avoidance of accountability, it is a "deepening" of accountability to meet newly discernible imperatives.

As Lovelace himself pointed out, "the much vaunted cultural creativity expressed in Trinidad and Tobago has come principally from the ordinary African-descended people at the bottom of the economic ladder." It was his way of rejecting the northward climb for power at the top of the pyramid—for to occupy the top of a pyramid is to occupy a very small space indeed.

•

11 Glissant, in his 1997 book *Poetics of Relation*, discusses the concept of the "right to opacity," arguing that marginalized groups should have the right to not be fully understood or transparent. See: Édouard Glissant, *Poetics of Relation*, trans. Betsy Wing (University of Michigan Press, 1997).

12 Cameroonian philosopher Achille Mbembe's seminal contribution to, and complication of, Foucault's biopolitics comes as the term *necropolitics*, which speaks about the kind of sociopolitical power that marks some bodies out as deserving of death. See: Achille Mbembe, *Necropolitics*, trans. Steven Corcoran (Duke University Press, 2019).

•

In a fascinating and popular tale told by the Brothers Grimm, published in 1812, an old hardworking shoemaker and his wife fall on very hard times.

Down to their last strap of leather, barely enough to make a pair of shoes, and with their bellies sprouting cobwebs, they retire for the night—not knowing what the next day might bring. In the morning, instead of a mournful patch of leather staring back at his tired eyes, the shoemaker lands his gaze on the finest pair of shoes he has seen in a good while. During the day, he is able to sell the pair to an eager customer who fancies his feet more than he does his purse, paying the grateful cobbler more than is normally due.

Stumped by his sudden fortune, but delighted to be able to afford more leather to make more shoes, the shoemaker makes a purchase, reverently and quizzically arranges the patches on his worktable, and retires for the night. When the sun rises, it shines its goodness upon even more shoes. New shoes. Perhaps more beautiful than the last pair. Desiring to return the favor to their invisible benefactor, the revitalized couple stay up late, peeping from the shadows, only to find to their eternal shock two small naked men sneak into their store, gather the materials, toil and sweat for hours, and cobble together new pairs of shoes.

I remembered this story quite fondly when I read about Rodney Holbrook, seventy-five years old, retired postman, and resident of Builth Wells, Powys, in Wales. Rodney and his wife woke up every morning to find their shed cleaner than he left it. *BBC News* reports what Rodney did to solve the mystery: "After regularly discovering that things from the night before had been mysteriously tidied, he set up a night vision camera on his workbench." The footage he obtained depicted a house-proud mouse dutifully clearing away things, diligently putting them away, keeping the Holbrook household clean in its scurrying business.

"I don't bother to tidy up now, I leave things out of the box and they put it back in its place by the morning," Rodney remarked to the BBC.

"I think he would tidy my wife away if I left her in there."

Like the fictional "elves" in the cobbler tale, and the red-eye mouse in the Holbrook footage, there were once Black slaves who carried away the fecal matter of the more prestigious residents in Rio de Janeiro, Brazil. They were the aspiring city's inaugural public latrine system. Their bodies were so marked by their terrible task that their skins curdled into gnarled stripes and leathery hisses, earning them the nickname *tigres* (tigers). But it mattered little what they were called. To the city, which longed to replicate the metropolitan successes of European counterparts, when its eminent inhabitants sought to take a shit, hidden figures were there to cart away their blush, their bodies metabolizing the abjection of the discarded.

The neurotypical marks the expectation that when we walk, when our feet land on the ground, our footsteps will be upheld by the ground's sturdiness. You might think of this expectation as a simple faith, an anticipatory modality necessary to the business of living. Switch on a phone and dial a number? Why, that mere act—by the very "laws of nature"—should summon an expected other! Nothing to it. It's merely "practical." But even this "simple faith" is political, shrouding an uneasy entitlement that is subsidized by hidden figures, curdled skin, rodent imperatives, and bodies that live in the fissures of the dominant tendencies that make up the familiar.

Phones don't "merely" work; they often trace out cartographies that are ignited by the bodies of Congolese boys mining cobalt to power batteries and telephonic conversations. Donuts don't "simply" taste good; their saccharine sweetness enmeshes the decimation of Malaysian and Indonesian forests, which in turn powers vegetable oil production necessary for frying the pastries. And shit doesn't just disappear.

Behind the curtains of the sensorial familiar, tucked within the folds of habituated expectations, nourishing the ritual of entitlement, backgrounded by the vicissitudes of common sense, are hidden lives and hidden deaths. Hidden arrangements. Something wide-eyed and queerly breathing. Prosthetic bodies rendered abject, unpronounceable, outside the thesis of the useful.

But then once in a while, the shockwaves of syncopation travel through the city, upsetting the neat order of the senses, upturning the aesthetics of the polite: postman meets rat; cobbler meets elves; citizen meets vagabond. And civilization meets its monsters. We could rehabilitate those monsters when we meet them. You know, pull them into the hospitality of inclusivity. A more thrilling prospect is one of radical accompaniment, dancing with the monstrous into stranger solidarities. Into the cracks where miracles are bred.

•

•

Forgiveness is settling debts; reconciliation is troubling boundaries.

•

•

In the part of the world where I grew up, we regularly made appointments to meet with God once every week. We opened his vast chambers on Sundays, and into those celebrated walls we flocked like black sheep longing to be shorn of our excess wool.

The sanctuary decorators and keepers took certain pains to make the stage where the "man of God" stood and spoke as the mouthpiece of the divine as commandingly majestic and rapturous as they possibly could. And when the work was done, when the speaking was complete and the words delivered, we would leave our wool scattered among the pews in the wake of our Lord's shearing—happy to be free of our burdens. Happy to be made whole.

We did this for years. Without fail. Every Sunday. Sometimes on Wednesdays for the more spiritual ones among us. We would come. The doors would be open. God would be there—or so we were told—and we would bask in the afterglow of his majestic inscrutability and sacred unquestionability. I however had plenty of questions. I often worried how he was doing, if he was keeping well being locked up behind the fabric of our anxious seeking, being harangued with our constant praise and prayers. Being "God." But he just sat there, barely perceptible in the curious shapes of the dust storms our stomping feet whipped up in the roofed tabernacle. Strangely regular and well-behaved.

He never failed at showing up.
Until he did.

I can't remember the day or the moment, but I distinctly remember arriving at the ornate doorsteps of the sanctuary, sitting myself in the chair, and feeling that God wasn't there. He had slipped away, leapt over the fence, shed his embroidered robes, and run mad and naked into the wilderness. No one else seemed to notice. They just went on as usual, stomping up dust storms, screaming loudly, adoring him with all his usual names—leaving the sacred behind them as soon as the last benediction was uttered and the Grace shared. Back to the ordinary they went. The rankling, deadening familiar.

For me, his footsteps still glowed seductively in the rough sands where he had declared his freedom. His clothes marked the spot where he slipped away, no longer hesitant about what he had done. His great sin: re-enchanting the ordinary. His sacrilegious act: changing his name and address to—everywhere. No longer the irrepressibly transcendent one, but the diffractively immanent manifold. No longer the one who sits at the end of the straight and narrow, but at the crossroads—the intersection where things are confused, where things meet, where things shapeshift. No longer the Sphinxian figure who solves all our problems, or even the one who asks new questions, but the one who muddies the water. The confounding variable. No longer the omnipresent, or the omni-absent, but the omni-emergent. The omni-imminent. The one always yet to come. Yet to happen. The one who slips away.

I have sought "him" ever since. In the glistening eyes of my wife. In the tantrums of our children. In the joyful moment the tap water pierces through the air and hits the stained dish. In the rippling of a Chennai dawn. Through the permeable membrane of a flying fox's outspread wings. At the very instant the tiny countdown on a YouTube ad becomes "Skip Ad." Under boring rocks. In the sticky folds of my hypocrisies. In the moment the right words become apparent. And especially in those moments when words are no longer useful.

When others ask me why I do not show up on Sundays, I often say, under my breath, "But what about Mondays ... and Thor's days?" I often try to tell them about this confounding notion of "god"—about this bubbling spring that wells up in the cracks of the ordinary, urging us to notice the world anew. I want to tell them about a vaster sanctuary I am coming to know: not one where you walk in broken and leave mended, but one where you walk in mended and leave broken. Where you walk in eloquent and leave with a lisp. Where the cavorting gait of the confident is disciplined by the hand of god upon the thigh—dislodging the bones. I want to tell them that in these times of painful losses, of starving bellies and emaciated hopes, where the lingering spectacle of destruction shadows the lands, and the story of our godhood still gnaws at the bones of the world, we cannot afford those knowledges that presume our superiority. We cannot practice escape any longer—if we are to survive. We cannot cleanse ourselves of our sins or hope for the parting of the clouds to bring a convenient savior. I want to tell them that "god" has left the building and we must now gesture toward hopes and worlds beyond modern imaginaries. Beyond humans. Beyond the intelligible. Beyond our usual ways of making sense. I want to tell them that we must go to the edges in the middle, toward the hedgerows teeming with haggadays and gargoyles and stuttered beings, and learn to withness the world we once banished to the peripheries of significance.

•

•

I'm almost tempted to say that the fragments of poetry are prose becoming autistic.
—Ralph Savarese

Poetry is prose becoming autistic. There are worlds of significance in this remark.

First, poetry is more than just meter and rhyme. Rather, poetry is a response to the hidden tensions in expression itself. That is, words are not perfectly still, resolute in their meanings, fully themselves all by themselves. A word is not fully disclosed by its definition. Indeed, definitions can often obscure what words are doing. Words only show up in part.

If we think about autism beyond its usual diagnostic designations, as a flowing that travels alongside the main, as the crack that precedes the object, then poetry is the outworking of those minor tendencies that unsettle the stability of words. Not content with meaning, not content with definition, not content with formal structure, poetry irrupts where prose is satisfied with smooth, linear trajectories. Expression's hidden mistress.

It might be equally powerful to note that these errant lines that trace out poetic gestures are the condition for expression. Yes. Poetry precedes words. Precedes language. Poetry is not a type of expression; it is expression's condition of expressivity. The moonlit wolf's howl that evolutionarily transmutes itself into expressions of human anxiety, inspiring all the words that we now associate with dread and fear, is reducible to neither wolf nor human. Something in the field flutters, trembles, quakes, and gestures into language.

This must be what my wife means when she—observing our autistic son Kyah in his occasional silence—says: "Even when he is silent, he is singing worlds."

•

•

I often think that memory is bigger than my head. Or my body. And that it envelops my corporeal members; along with reluctant and desirous others; along with the bright and joyfully-fonted colors scratched out on faint blue lines in an old exercise book; along with blistered images of mushroom clouds filtered through haunting sepia; in a mad dance of alien becomings. Some bizarre kind of cartography, probably, this memory.

Is the Atlantic a memory, more than just a reference? Could it be that when I remember something, I am different every time the memory glows? Could it be that to remember is to be re-membered?

•

•

Bones bend spacetime. One must move slowly with them, slowly as they themselves move. Whether it is the bones of diatoms flowing across the Atlantic Ocean in processual plumes of life-giving dust, or the ancient bones of creatures we can only imagine today, bones are dense materialities—inviting prophecy, not pity. Inviting us to look again, inviting miracles, inviting slowing down.

Slowing down is thus about lingering in the places we are not used to. Seeking out new questions. Becoming accountable to more than what rests on the surface. Seeking roots. Slowing down is taking care of ghosts, hugging monsters, sharing silence, embracing the weird.

Slowing down is meeting the sensuous. The idea of slowing down is not about getting answers, it is about questioning our questions. It is about staying in the places that are haunted.

It is about uncovering bones.

•

•

When there is trouble, darkness extinguishes the light not only to mark the occasion, but to broadcast a creative event—the birth of something new.

Around 42,000 years ago, or so the stories tattooed on kauri tree bodies seem to tell us, the world ended. It must have felt sudden: aurorae dancing in the mid-heavens like murmurations of fairies let loose upon the planet; the death of megafauna; a radical uptick in atmospheric radiocarbon levels leading to death of Neanderthals. An apocalypse.

Researchers in Australia looking today at the stories carved into ancient kauri tree stumps tell us that the earth experienced a magnetic field reversal, temporarily flipping the north and south poles, exposing the planet to solar winds. The cosmic storm, once called the Laschamps Excursion, and now christened the Adams Transitory Geomagnetic Event, led to mass extinction events that drove human populations deeper into the dark, beneath the surface of things, where they hid and created cave art we still see today.

There in the belly of the earth, in the amniotic dark, this unnamed neonate collective learned to see. Learned to weave new trust coalitions.

Seeing in the dark is a critical capacity needed in times of trouble. Today, as viral winds blow and the protection of the modern shrivels in the face of fierce topographical shifts, the darkness, like an old friend, like a familiar griot, screams in the town square: it is time to shapeshift.

•

•

These are the days of wandering oxymorons. These are the times we must seek out the contrary, the paradoxical, the distant, the impossible, and the counterintuitive. To find brighter light, we must head for the gloomiest caves; to understand ourselves, we must turn to the strange; to find the way out of our troubles, we must embrace them with fonder reverence, and to thrive... to live, we must come to the thinnest places, where life and death aren't opposites but bedfellows.

•

•

Modernity didn't get rid of the sacred. It relocated the sacred by confining it to the coordinates of the human—notably the white male body, its chiefest avatar. Here, within the vortices of the post/modern rejection of an authorial world beyond humans, within the anthropological project, lies a temple dedicated to the worship of categories, progress, mastery, and Icarian flight. In some way or the other, we are all—even those of us capable of critiquing this site of worship—enlisted to serve this arrangement of things, to clean the pews, to pass around the basket, to gape at the priests in the holiest of holies. But the sacred is not held down for long. Today, if you listen, you might hear the tense grip of the human beginning to soften as our claims to centrality flail against a compelling nonhuman argument. If you listen a bit longer, you might even discern the chaordic footfalls of the sacred migrating from its former abode, whistling as it coddiwomples down the asphalted remains of our failure to arrive.

•

•

In these fluid times, the soul has changed location: it is neither within, where our religious traditions mostly situated it, nor without, among the wondrous and presumably determined order of the material world, where the natural philosophers hid it. It is between—in ecologies of weird bodies and howling sounds and throbbing membranes and secreting liquids and alien hues and nightly migrancies. The hallowed interior is broken; the mute exterior breached. The soul is at large, off the record, beside itself, always-to-come. And all we are left with is a gasp.

•

•

It is a poor arrangement that pits magic against the mundane, urging us to imagine both as estranged aspects on either side of an unbridgeable rift. This arrangement is harmful to both concepts: as if magic were consigned to the spectacular, the supernatural, the incredible, the unserious, the impractical, and as if "the ordinary" were the painfully predictable motions of already determined things in their already determined orbits.

Magic is not the alien other of the quotidian but the resuscitation of the ordinary; the embarrassing excessiveness and mad intelligence of the world we presume we own; the crimson blush that fries the white face of assuredness. Magic is the unfinished-ness of things, the way things shrink away from being fully articulated and named; the way the resting surface of a taut drumhead still vibrates and spits quantum lyrics in defiance of our measuring instruments; the off-the-record-ness of an entangled and entangling world. To know magic is to touch our own bodies and realize that many universes curdle in the spell of that seemingly boring encounter. To know the ordinary is to be haunted by all the things it won't say.

•

•

What if we composted justice? What might we see, hear, touch, or sense when we, recovering from rectitude, lie flat on our backs, philosophers of the horizontal? What might a flat ecology teach us about an animal world of demise, desire, and determination? A world that exceeds the moral arc of Lutherian imagination? A world where justice often gets in the way of transformation?

What if we composted justice?

•

•

Trust is more than a feeling of confidence or a cognitive transaction that sprouts from within (or is limited to) the spaces between human selves. Instead, trust is the fidelity (or loss thereof) of a relationship between bodies that allows those bodies to dynamically respond to complex challenges. Two human best friends might trust each other, but this "feeling" is not exclusive to them or to sentient beings. An orchid and a wasp are in relationships of trust. The same might be said about the crocodile and the Egyptian plover bird, or a cow and the hard-working microbiota of methanogens in its gut that feed on the cow's ingested food and produce methane. In these nonhuman instances of trust—highlighting somatic economies of agency and response-ability, prosthetic arrangements of limbs and tentacles and flagella—a feeling isn't central to the phenomenon: what is of note is how these bodies deploy, delimit, define, disable, and dance each other. What might also be discerned is how distrust can be conceived as embodied avoidance, so that the things we turn away from mark us and are marked by us.

We are all in relationships of trust, most of which are nonconscious and unthought, widespread and diasporic. As perhaps the most singularly valuable currency to bodies in their manifold materialities, trust is how we live and die.

•

•

When we speak, our bodies speak. Our ancestors speak. Our bacteria speak. Our bodies are assemblages of other bodies, inseparable from the worlds and geologies and ecologies and materialities they are already entangled with. The communication theorists tried to think of an effective communicative event as the absence of "noise," but language is inherently noisy and indirect. Every speech act is teeming with many lives-deaths and many voices. Many other things are going on during an act of utterance that cannot be encoded as meaning.

•

•

The fugitive cannot afford to speak truth to power. Marronage, the act of removing oneself from the control of the slave plantation, wasn't preceded by honesty or truth-telling, but creative deception and a refusal of the epistemological imperatives of the master.

•

•

Long before he drew his last breath in 180 CE, Marcus Aurelius wrote these lines:

> *He is a true fugitive, that flies from reason by which men are sociable. He is blind who cannot see with the eyes of his understanding. He is poor that stands in need of another, and hath not in himself all things needful for this life. He is an apostate of the world, who by being discontented with those things that happen unto him in the world, doth as it were apostatize, and separate himself from common nature's rational administration ... He raises sedition in the city, who by irrational actions withdraws his own soul from that one and common soul of all rational creatures.*

The good emperor of Rome unwittingly (and helpfully, I might add!) offered a beautiful cartography of fugitivity. Note the ingredients: "flights from reason"; "dependence on senses other than just sight"; "needing others and living with a larger sense of abundance than self-sufficiency can comprehend"; "performs an apostasy of the city and its exclusive claims to power by seeking out other places of power"; and finally, "becomes unruly and ungovernable."

This is a recipe for the task of making sanctuary and midwifing a politics of becoming-animal. The joy of becoming response-able to something beyond the coherence of the city.

•

•

Poetry is the language of the apocalypse. When cracks appear, when tensions materialize and split the familiar open, the least thing you need is precision. The least thing you want is to simply get to the point. Well, the poet casts his eyes beside the point, beneath the surfaces, where the exquisite sprouts.

•

•

In this time of catastrophes followed by catastrophes, as novel viruses prowl the streets, as nation-states struggle to remain relevant political units in the face of geological and technological shifts, and as old rituals no longer ignite the warming fires by which our modern experiments have kept the cold at bay, an unearthly tune might be heard—wafting through the ruins of proud but anxious civilization, unsettling the browning leaves of disillusionment, whispering through traumascapes of exhausted activisms, braiding itself with the sinews of the migrant winds that once powered the sails of humanist progress and confidence.

This arrhythmic howl is by turns soft and bodacious, barely perceptible at times and then impossible to ignore. This "tune" is not music, and yet it is the irresistible stuff music is made of. If we listened, we might hear no discernible lyrics, no convenient message—and yet that is the point: this tune is our permission to fail, an invitation to new reformulations of citizenry. A call to delirious depths. What might failure look like? Where might this generative incapacitation lead us? Who are we and who is here with us? I do not know yet. But I suspect that as I try my feet and hips to these seditious sounds and throw my limbs in trust of the abundance of this place, I will be caught by the surprise of the many already dancing with me—for failure is rich, and where there is "nothing," there is much to go around.

•

•

Do not dishonor the stars by seeking to reach them, by trusting that home lies in the glittery distance. "Reaching for the stars" erases the hard work they have done, traveling unfathomable miles across our galaxy, spilling their guts in temper tantrums, baptizing earth with the very minerals that have become our bodies and our civilizations. Reaching for the stars? Why? They are already pressingly close, stirring with our bodies, tricksters of eternal night. We can learn that stars are "far" because they teach us that distance is not synonymous with separation. We can learn that the homes we seek are seductively near, here in the thick-now, some creative risks away from the familiar.

•

•

The sacred is not the shining thing at the end of the journey awaiting disclosure; the sacred is the journey: the celebrated departure and tearful goodbyes, the blue skies of optimism that dip in the welcoming horizons, the hint of gray in foreboding clouds, the obstacles that pepper the road with treacherous texture, the marauding doubts that steal your steps, the hallucinated masquerade that tortures your sleep, the glimpsed finish line, the exhausted arrival, and the morning after arrival when the meaning of home needs to be reiterated again and again. One does not approach the sacred: the approach is the sacred. The way to heaven is where heaven is.

You might say then: well, why not just get to the point and say that the sacred is "everything"? Why go through the trouble of being specific? It is because to speak of "everything" is a linguistic convenience that risks reinforcing the image of a static container world filled with static things with static properties. Such a world couldn't permit the sacred to exist. Instead, the "world" we live with/in is so ecstatically indeterminate in its becoming, so relationally fluid, so processually entangled, so exceeding in its promiscuity, that one must often hesitate to name it, to think of it as a "world" with finished "things." And that there is the "sacred," the radical incompleteness that haunts "things" and engulfs them in a murmuration of becoming that is too complex for language to represent. The fugitivity of all bodies-in-their-ongoingness.

The sacred is the wound on heaven's flesh.

•

•

When we act, we act-with-the-world. We act-with-community. We act-with-legacies-we-don't-even-know. We act-with-selves-that-haunt-our-independence. We act-with-others-because-we-are-hyphenated-bodies-that-are-often-difficult-to-decipher.

•

•

Ironically, making an appeal to our "common humanity" as a way of getting around the intractability of the race question reinforces racialized categories of thought. Such appeals are permeated with a costly universalism, one that requires bodies of all kinds to sustain its complicated claims to sublime heights; one that is constantly burdened with the need to pathologize deviations from its standards and to enforce difference (as if difference were an unfortunate thing).

Needless to say, I do not think stripping away "racial layers" means we will arrive at the "human" beneath, free from those loathsome burdens; there is no somatic purity underneath semiotic filth. The soma is already a political matter, a racial matter, a theological matter, an economic matter, a matter of loss and fortune and legacies and faith.

Instead of leaping into a presumably post-racial world, I'd rather invest in examining the ways the very concept, materialities, and contours of race are changing, transitioning, becoming different, becoming stranger: I'd like to sit at the crossroads where my black skin is both protecting my organs and participating in migrant planetary orgies of the fifth kind; I'd like the forbidden pleasures of a counter-modern politics that is capable of acknowledging that white identities are (and have historically been) granted creaturely comforts within globalizing/colonizing politico-economies (white settlements), while simultaneously noticing that "white identity" is not a metaphysical axiom or an inherited original sin, fixed in Euclidean spacetime, requiring salvation in a workshop or exhausting apologies—and that it too is volatile and transient with/in a world that is never settled.

More critically, I yearn for a politics of defamiliarization: a weird aesthetic that brings us close to the utter unspeakability of a world that exceeds our attempts to fix it, reduce it to intelligible terms, control it, or own it. A buck-toothed teenage world that reminds me of its awkward limbs and blushing attempts to be social. A politics that whispers to me that the meaning of race is yet to come.

•

•

We now live in fugitive times, and fugitive times require fugitive epistemologies, ways of knowing that stray from the modern addictions with representation. Deploying the settler epistemologies that contributed to the geo-ecological hostilities of the present risks reinforcing the dynamics we want to address. The promise of fugitivity, as we shall see, is that in a sense it helps resacralize the world, ministering to our weary bones by drawing "god" closer—so intimately close, in fact, that we lose some of the categorical independence modernity burdened us with.

One might say fugitivity is the theology of incalculability and hopelessness. The fugitive rejects the promise of repair and refuses the hope of the established order. By clinging to outlawed desires, barely perceptible imaginations, alien gestures, the fugitive inhabits the moving wilds. They live in open spaces, with rogue planets and stars astride a curious sky, in the tense betweenness of things.

God, surprisingly in love with the fugitive, often meets the fugitive in that space between stories to break him open, to show him a burning bush, to rename him, to gobble him up with mouth as wide as a whale's, and then perhaps to spit him out again. Fugitivity is the site of hopelessness, of so-called defeat, of modest bearings and whispered songs. For citizens of the Anthropocene, who must meet the incomprehensibility of the moment, the fugitive's path glows in the dark. There, where the path in the call to defeat leads, we might come face to face with something deeper than solutions. Something too sacred for words to embrace.

•

•

Faith is the fidelity of entanglements. Faith exceeds the doctrines and the human-centric ways we—forced by the imperatives of institutions—have come to see them. It is how bodies come to meet other bodies, how bodies use or borrow other bodies and senses to respond to the creative challenges of a multidimensional reality that is never still, or how those bodies in excess of each other create new edges and experiment with new questions.

You might even think of faith as symbiosis or sympoiesis: faith is the relationship between microbial civilizations in our guts and the memories we process. The water buffalo is the *kasaya* of the oxpecker; the ostrich is the yarmulke of the zebra. Faith means that bodies need bodies in order to thrive and in order to die well. It is coalitional, alliance-making, world-shaping, co-creative work. One does not have faith as such: we live and breathe and die in faith.

Faith does not terminate at binary truth statements or axioms. To make faith a subject of an ultimate truth, by which its value can be estimated, is to occlude the reality-forming work of faith. The question isn't whether my faith is "true" or not, nor whether the strangers outside our temples have the "right" faith. What's more urgent invites us into a consideration of what an ecosystem of faith is doing—what specific species of yearning are producing, what imaginal possibilities are proliferated and from what soil, what archetypes are being played with, and how bodies are assuming and losing shape. Faith is a fragile network of doings-together, a strategy of co-inquiry, experiments of approach where arrival is impossible.

In this sense, no "one" is reducible to the discernible contents of their faith practices or expressed beliefs and rituals. There's always something more, something excessive, something molecularly transgressive that upsets the firm rhetoric of faith-as-declaration. It is like removing a clean cobblestone and finding beneath it slimy worlds and critters unmentionable, doing their own business.

Faith is therefore revolutionary and has counter-imperial potentials. When we come to touch our faith, we come into an adventurous, expansive relationship with the bodies that are assembled in excess of ours. We touch the limbs of faith by listening to the materials, the memories, the furniture, the textures that are the condition of our becoming-with-the-world. In touching, we attune ourselves to how strange and alien we are, how composite our bodies are, how indebted we are, and how fugitive we are from systems of neat classification.

Faith is making sanctuary.

•

•

History is not what happened in the past; history is what we are doing right now to situate ourselves in the cross-currents of manifold temporalities. In this sense, history is an ongoing dynamic, a contemporary effort from which past and future are secreted, always closer than it appears to be.

How we perform history can tell us more about ourselves today than the past worlds we attempt to summon for our perusal. When we stress the stories of heroes past but leave out the tales of the monsters gestating in their guts, that's how we reinforce our visions of our anticipated futures. That's how we tell each other what to hope for, what to emulate, what to reproduce, what to learn from. We don't come from the past; we are made in the thick present, us and the origin stories we immortalize in the here and now.

•

•

We (humans, that is) are geological processes, intimately stratified with layers of soil, potentially discoverable by intelligences in the deep future as a troubling sedimentation of plastic and selfies; we are extractive practices, forceful settlements, archetypal longings, historical conflicts, microbial activisms, spacetime configurations, and climatic conditions—in their ongoing becoming. Our bodies are porous traffickings of movements. We don't live on the planet; we are the planet in its ongoing de/materialization.

•

•

It is commendable that we recognize that the world is not disposable, not just a plaything for our performances of forward movement, and that it stakes its own claims to agency and power—qualities we usually reserve for ourselves.

Now we must also acknowledge that we will not save the world.

To attempt to save the world is to render it—strange as it seems—eminently disposable. For in the effort to save it, however well-intentioned, we simultaneously position ourselves "outside" of material rhythms of transience that mobilize all things in fluid comings and goings. We perpetuate the myth of complete repair, the very storyline of colonial progress that encourages us to look past foreclosures, past endings, past lingering oppressions, into a promissory future where everything is set right.

Moreover, our previous efforts at trying to save the world are part of what has brought us here.

•

•

In his 1949 tome *The Hero with a Thousand Faces*, Joseph Campbell synthesizes his outrageously influential mythic model of the hero's journey: a complex, multi-stage narrative progression that begins with an ordinary person called into an adventure, being aided by a wiser elder, crossing a threshold (a point of no return), facing a series of critical tests, descending into the darkest cave, facing an ultimate monster in a most challenging ordeal, being rewarded with a lesson/sword/gift, and then—in the climax—reemerging in triumph.

The hero's journey is Rocky bouncing up the seventy-two steps of the Philadelphia Museum of Art in that famous training montage in *Rocky*; it is Frodo Baggins and Samwise Gamgee approaching the black gates of Mordor with the Ring of Power; it is Luke Skywalker crashing on Planet Dagobah where he meets the exiled Yoda, who will teach him how to use the Force. It is the Marvel Cinematic Universe's Avengers and probably every Disney movie in existence. The formula is so pervasive, so recognizable, and so resilient that it has become the de facto template through which we story and interpret our experiences—both personal and collective.

But, of course, Campbell's hero's journey has long-identified problems, starting with its claims to universal applicability (a claim which some argue stems from Campbell's white supremacist views,[13] though others repudiate these assertions) and the way Campbell seems to force different cultural patterns into his constellation of meaning. For me, the more damning assessment (not unrelated to the previous critiques) is the anthropocentrism of his model: the hero's journey is told exclusively from the hero's perspective. There's nothing wrong with that. However, in a world where meaning is neither stable nor the especial preserve of human actors, a lot is cut out that might be interesting to sit with. It is

---

13 See Brendan Gill, "The Faces of Joseph Campbell," *New York Review of Books*, September 28, 1989, and Robert A. Segal, "Joseph Campbell on Jews and Judaism," *Religion* 22, no. 2 (April 1992): 151–170.

as Nigerian author Chinua Achebe once said: "Until the lions have their own historians, the history of the hunt will always glorify the hunter."

I wonder what the monster thinks about the hero's journey. Perhaps the dramatic winds and themes that drive the hero-to-be from his ordinary origins towards the sulphuric depths where he will encounter his nemesis are perplexing to the monster. Perhaps the monster is the least concerned about the binary scenario the hero is locked into—victory or defeat—and simply wants to perform other rituals and imperatives. Perhaps one cannot "kill" the monster, since what it means to die and to live (the modern assumptions we hold about death) are not fixed across bodies or biological configurations. There are stories where the triumph of the hero (and the death of the monster) turns out to have been part of the monster's scheme all along. There are third and final acts in cinematic stories where the alien-defeating hero, swamped by the congratulations and festivities of a triumphant arrival, suddenly doubles over in intense pain and vomits. Aware of the concerned eyes that now fix their existential queries on him, he stands erect and reassures everyone of his good health, just as the camera closes in on him, revealing to the wide-eyed audience an alien presence gestating in his belly, a haunting stowaway in the narrative of victory.

This embarrassing excessiveness of things, this breaking-open of the anthropocentric model, this disruption of binaries, this inflection of the hero (wherein the hero becomes the "villain" or the vessel for the proliferation of monstrosity), is an invitation to humility. An invitation to examine our own claims to triumph. An invitation to listen to other imperatives beyond the village din of victory. I can think of no better example or figure than the alien-inseminated conqueror, the queered body of the hero, the fugitive fetus, to exemplify the central thesis of postactivism: the way we respond to the crisis, the way we attempt to defeat the monster, is the crisis.

•

•

Sacred/Profane. Good/Evil. Heterosexual/Homosexual. Man/Woman. This/That. Modernity's adamant proliferation of binaries often leaves us thinking there are only two ways to think about justice and activism: either we are "in" or we are "out." Inclusion/Exclusion. What this habitual persuasion occludes are the worlds between polarities. I am convinced that another operation is possible, another move is feasible. It involves cannibalizing these noxious dualisms and touching the worlds that have been socialized out of view by human centrism. It involves becoming-monster.

Monsters are neither in nor out—they are enactments of an "exteriority within," resisting being and embracing becoming. To become-monster is to become indiscernible to surveillance systems; it is to hide, to move swiftly, to become dis-organ-ized, to become scattered, to become-favela. In awkward times, we need a weird politics that invites us to become-awkward, to think like crossroads, to lose our way, to come apart, and to perhaps make differences in ways that disrupt the ongoing ensorcellment of modern closure.

•

What if the ways we converse with each other, the polarities we assemble behind, and the terms that frame our explorations and imaginations are processual extensions of the nation-state? What if our bodies are so interpenetrated by powerful regimes of thought and control that even our attempts at freedom are already anticipated, already categorized, already part of the program? What if we are the powers-that-be we oppose, and in the performance of dissent we inadvertently legitimize the structures we pray to dismantle?

What then?

•

When you get to the end of the tunnel where the light awaits, don't walk off rudely into his arms. Turn towards the smoldering darkness whence you came, and thank her for shaping you, for scaring you, for wounding you, and defeating you, and shaking you, because in her womb you were thoroughly purged, and made fresh for new glimpses of wonder. And as you walk further into the domineering light, the dark will bless you with a gift to remind you that you are not as contained or as limited as you think, that there is more to you than what meets the educated eye, that whatever you do, the whole universe does the same along with you—imitating you with a childish keenness, and that you are never ever alone. That's why shadows were invented.

•

•

We do not feel emotions as much as we are bent into shapes by open-ended territories of feeling. Affective states are not individual events, quarantined within human bodies, lining up with predetermined neural networks that track unto recognizable physiological manifestations. Instead the "things" we call "emotions" are principalities and powers at large that enlist bodies of all kinds in their mattering. Affective assemblages. Large territorial beasts with human bodies as organelles.

To feel is to glow; it is to be activated at the crossroads where politics, expectations, stories, bodies, furniture, media, food, spirits, computational frameworks of neoliberalism, history, and microbial worlds intra-sect. Decentering humans from the story of feeling relieves us from the burden of emotional authenticity, and might open up post-qualitative research adventures to the edges of sentimentality. More importantly, it can tell us a lot about the territories we are entangled with, creating the conditions within which we might begin to appreciate how habitual modes of feeling can often get in the way of our flourishing.

In other words: in our search for the unusual, for the unspoken, for sanctuary, we must keep in mind—the new may not feel right.

•

•

If the human eye were fully committed to image identification, it would leave no spot untouched, no stone unturned, in its quest to translate all the light that the cornea focuses on the retinal cells into a visual field. The eye is, however, not entirely entranced by the prospects of sight. A tithe of the light that flows through the iris falls on the eye's optic disc, which is the point where the ganglion cells become a tunneling nerve that leaves the eye and travels towards the brain's occipital lobe. This point of departure is the blind spot. The blind spot means we can't see everything, and yet without the blind spot we can't see anything. To see is to leave something out. And what a gift that is! The blind spot is the *beresheit*[14] of the visual apparatus. If we didn't have blind spots, we would probably be incarcerated in a panopticon of vision from which no escape would be possible. Our blind spots relieve us of the burden of figuring everything out. They queer the biological notion of sight, making it not so much a matter of representation as a fluid performance of

---

14 The written Torah opens with the term *beresheit*, which is usually interpreted as "In the beginning." But something more interesting than accounts of stable origins is going on. Beresheit seems to be more an apophatic mark of radical openness, more a crack than a stentorian declaration of authorship. Karen Barad writes (in her chapter in *Entangled Worlds*):

> *The great medieval Torah commentator Rashi warns: Do not read the opening line of Genesis as "In the beginning God created the heavens and the earth..."* because this is not what the Hebrew says. *[Emphasis mine.] In fact, the grammatical construction of the opening sentence of Torah doesn't make sense.* B'reishit, *the first word, is in "construct form," meaning that it should be the first of two nouns in a row, that would be translated: [the first noun] of [the second noun], as in* B'nei Yisrael, *"the children of Israel."* B'reishit *thus means "in [a/the] beginning of..." and there is no noun that directly follows. In fact, Rashi writes: "This verse says nothing but* darsheini*—'Expound me!'" That is, according to Rashi, the opening word of the Torah is just that: an opening—an invitation to interpret; it is in effect an injunction against the very possibility of literal interpretations of the Bible... The opening is nothing but an emphasis on the text's ongoing openness: on the lack of determinacy. Creation is an indeterminate matter. And the first word of the Torah, what seems to start out as the articulation of a beginning, uses the word "beginning" in such a way that it interrupts itself to question the very possibility of origin, linear temporality, determinism, and determinacy.*

See: Karen Barad, "What Flashes Up: Theological-Political-Scientific Fragments," in *Entangled Worlds: Religion, Science, and New Materialisms*, eds. Catherine Keller and Mary-Jane Rubenstein (Fordham University Press, 2017), 21–88.

little bodies. They ground us in a world of play and necessary shadows. And they offer a cautionary lesson: if you know the whole thing, if you are so confident in your answers that you dismiss their indebtedness to context, if you have arrived, if you can see everything, you've already missed a spot.

•

•

"Chicken or the egg? Which came first?"

A decade ago, scientists decided they had finally resolved the age-old philosophical riddle: chicken! They discovered ovocleidin-17, the protein found only in chickens that is responsible for converting calcium carbonate into calcite crystals, which make up the eggy outer shell membrane necessary for embryonic development.

Some evolutionary biologists are not so sure though. They point to the evolutionary tree, and suggest that eggs did come before chickens: the First One True Chicken had to have been born as the mutated offspring of Almost-Chickens, and was very likely born via egg—since that reproductive technology had been available to other species millions of years prior.

Between ovocleidin-17 and evolutionary trees, we seem stuck with which came first, irreparably lost in the persistent cyclicity of absurdity that comes with arborescent thinking.

There's another way to think of the riddle. When we think in terms of which came first, we prioritize an anthropocentric analysis in a world that is majestically more complicated than such arboreal models of ordinance and sequential progression. Instead of reiterating the imperatives of arborescence and originals, I think with the DeleuzoGuattarian figure of the rhizome, and with Barad's concept of intra-action.

Within a rhizome, hierarchical privileges are not essential. Things don't predate other things in a neat uncontroversial way. Intra-action notes that the world is not populated by things with already determined properties interacting with other static subjects. Intra-action means that only in the context of relationships do things gain their thinginess. Much in the same way that a newborn baby births her mother by making her a mother, and similar to the way a book has no length until a measurement is made (intra-acting with a ruler) and not prior, the chicken and the egg are not separate entities. They gain their haecceity only in the mutuality of their encounter: the chicken only becomes a chicken in the moment the egg is enacted as an egg. No one comes first.

But that's not a fixed solution to the riddle. Other answers are possible. To think rhizomatically is not to arrive at some loftier answer or truth—it is to notice that the methods we deploy to research the world, its chickens and eggs, produce certain realities to the exclusion of others. How we look and move in the world cocreates the real. If you prioritize ovocleidin-17 and creationist ideas, you'd likely arrive on the chicken-first thesis. And if you intra-act with evolutionary biology, you're likely on the eggy side of things.

Which is true? Truth is the proprioceptive luxury of sedentary, upright-postured humans—and not some ultimate archive of events. The world spills away, folds away from final analyses and confident resolutions. Chicken or egg? Depends on how you look at it and what assemblage is enabling your analysis. I'm hungry.

•

•

Could language be doing more than communicating shared meaning? Is there something about the materiality of speech that escapes the trap of intelligibility? What if the hissing, clicking, licking, spitting, glossal, alveolar, muscular movements that are the conditions of speech are igniting processes other than doing what we convene them to do?

If that's the case, language exceeds its truth value. Words, once shot out from the lips of a sender, do not expire at the gates of the receiver or in the hallways of perception. They carry on worlding the world long after we are through with them, sneaking past our anxieties about what's true and what's not, evaporating into cloud-shaped clouds, descending into rich soil, sedimenting into ancient layers of grief, cavorting with fungal communities, sporulating into ant heads, exploding into the alchemy of fruit, which is then plucked by a weary author suffering from writer's block, whose generous bite into said fruit recognizes something molecular that makes his eyes widen and his heart race.

•

•

We must relinquish our convenient narratives of human exceptionalism and triumphalism—those stories that centralize human agency and enthrone human interests as supremely paramount in the multiverse. And we must do this not simply because we are now regaining some awareness about the nobility of other species and life forms—and not entirely because we are ourselves now humbled by our less than spectacular origins, but mainly because these times of upheaval call on us to revisit what is implied in being human. Do we continue to insist that we are lords over all, masters of the universe—uniquely distanced from the fleshy, dirty discourses of "nature"—ravaging plagues burning soil and earth into asphalted forms of our own making? Or do we recognize our relatedness to all things, our real dependence on the land we supposedly transcend, and that to be human is not a magisterial decree of isolation, but a chorus ... a syncretic process of shared ecological participation?

•

•

Nothing is independent or preexistent. Everything is hyphenated. And this is perhaps the most shocking realization of the modern human: that his skin and his sentience are not the taut boundaries that separate him from the brute; that the estranged "other," the diseased infidel, and the foreigner are the condition that makes his own existence possible; and that when he peers into his own soul, it is not a full stop, a decimal place, or an exclamation mark he finds, but an intriguing ellipsis attached to a sentence that is always changing.

•

•

Mothering is not just the unilinearity of procreation, the duplication of familiar shapes and forms along a single genomic track. S/he exceeds that. S/he is richer, more promiscuous, than that.

In Yorubaland, in the homeland and in the diaspora, many still speak of and venerate Yemoja, the supreme orisha whose name means "Mother whose children are the fish" (and if you were to travel to Abeokuta in Southwest Nigeria, you are likely to come across people with facial scars like fish gills slashed across their cheeks).

Yemoja is believed to be the first Mother, the womb that spat out the other notable orishas worshipped in Nigeria and across the Atlantic. But her motherhood is queer and unwieldy, perhaps monstrous: many *itan* or story-poems about Yemoja say she has no children of her own, but her breasts are notably long because she spends her time breast-feeding children. The other gods mocked Yemoja's long breasts and she ran away in her trauma, transforming into a river. Yemoja is thus the amniotic fluid that rushes and flows and froths with trauma and love and longing and the pain of watery becomings, the matrixial web that collects everything and enlists us all in a murmuring cacophony of surprise.

This idea that the mother is more than just an exclusive identity, a tight-lipped category, or a stable archetype is hinted at in the phenomenon of microchimerism, in which biologists observe that pregnant women do not merely propagate cells towards their fetuses but also receive cells from them. This bidirectional transfer of cells constitutes a co-mothering dynamic that continues even after the first baby is born, rippling through the bodies of siblings that come afterwards (in a sense, if you are an older sibling, you are in some senses part of the mothering of your younger sibling). Mothering, read through Indigenous Yoruba lenses and newer biological insights, becomes more than just static reproduction—it becomes a vocation of body-sharing practices, a transcorporeal fellowship, a bequeathing of trembling, a riverine melting into each other. A destabilizing of foundations. A fleshly way the world (if we could ever speak of a "world") whispers to itself, "I don't know."

•

•

One of my disappointments with academic life was being told that I ought to be more "factual," and lose the lyricism of my voice. No one read the data or had patience enough to go through boring statistical compilations, but somehow, it was the legitimate thing to do as a researcher: to keep producing boring bits of data no one had the time to read thoroughly. I wanted to do something different. And I did.

I remember being told by my wonderful doctoral panel that I had written beautifully, and communicated in a way that captured attention about the very complex shamanic narratives I investigated. Then one panel member suggested that this was in fact the problem with my work: "Your work should be based on fact. Science is about fact, not stories."

I understand these sentiments well. We live in a world that treats language and experience as a bifurcation between what is true and what is not true, what is here versus what is there, and, more to the point, what is fact and what is fiction or what "comes from the heart" and what "comes from the head." We depend on these binaries to navigate through the deep ambiguities of life. It's how we make sense of the world. So, when someone comes along speaking about life and butterflies and cosmic parliaments, it excites imagination—but then we neatly categorize those words as "poetry." A more entangled perspective, I think, is embodied in the recognition that everything is poetry. There isn't a factual world, where everything is data and stone—as opposed to a poetic world with blushing skies and raging seas.

Perhaps I should rephrase that: everything is poetic. Poetry is usually associated with rhyme and meter, figures of speech, and exciting turns of phrase. The poetic, however, is experience that is humble in the face of what can be known or what is im/possible. It is mystery, wonder—tactile, sensuous, and carnal. When you consider how paradoxical reality is, how we secrete our own knowledge production systems, how data is never neutral but actually a cultural artifact, how plural and prodigious "human" experiences are, you might begin to sense what I often call "the poetics of the preposterous." Nothing is given. Not origin, or destiny, or time, or space, or spacetime, or cause, or effect, or seed-time, or harvest, or death. It was this sense of mystery that gave birth to our sciences. And nay! Not just the sciences. To language itself!

Is mathematics some kind of stoic, gray language of the universe? Is quantum physics the study of the obvious? Is physics or theology or anything that we can come up with (whether or not it fits disciplinary modes of thought) "factual"? I think not. No one encounters the world as it is. Experience is material co-creation. The world isn't out there, with fixed boundaries and unyielding values, awaiting objective discovery. We cocreate it in every moment, rethinking its configurations, shifting walls, destroying and reinforcing, over and over again. As opposed to the notion of a cosmos that is still, containing a definite "amount" of knowledge that we would do very well to drink up, we "live in" a cosmos that resists any sort of finality—one that was once created, and has never been; one that is circumscribable as well as spontaneous. A universe entangled, stern, playful, terrible, and beautiful.

Of course, this does not suggest that the kind of information that is popularly viewed as "factual" doesn't serve certain ends. If a community has been devastated by terrorists or geological events, you may want to know how many people lost their lives, and would probably be put off if someone responded by speaking about "thin veils between worlds" and "souls in flight." Certain contexts call for different modes of speaking. The point to note here, however, is that the way we make meaning of our experiences is itself produced by deep cultural biases and imperatives, which inform us that when things sound poetic, they are probably useless (or good only for inspirational moments), and that when someone is "factual," he is striking at the heart of the universe. What slips past us is that physics, data, and numbers are "stories"—and just as groundless as Shakespearean tongue.

Describing life as "the condition that distinguishes animals and plants from inorganic matter, including the capacity for growth, reproduction, functional activity, and continual change preceding death" is high poetry, deeply steeped in metaphor, religious philosophy, a sense of beauty, and a sense of hope. It is no more powerful than saying "life is a canoe, wafting through wary streams." If what you "know" isn't a place of contest, a struggle, then what you "know" is dead.

•

•

There are perhaps two ways to positively respond to a question. The first is to offer a resolution. The other is to offer a rite of passage. In the former, an answer is given that reinforces the question in the same economy of ideas and relationships that were its first conditions. In the latter, the question is composted, reframed, ceremonially removed from its initiating conditions by means of bewilderment until the question meets itself and no longer feels the urgency of resolution. It is how the biblical God responded to Job when the latter prayed for an answer to his theodicean queries about suffering and goodness. It is how Esu, the Yoruba trickster, answered the prayers of the slaves across the Atlantic as he traveled through their rite of passage that we now call the Middle Passage. It is perhaps how we are being invited to meet the world today in the midst of our unfolding. Something more than a resolution wants to happen.

•

•

A significant part of the work of fugitivity is naming the plantation. Exile begins here. These days are the days of exile, not escape—since escape often reinforces the power arrangements we find problematic. In exile, we refuse to let central power be central; we undercut power's claims to exclusivity. In halting steps of deep experimentation and inquiry replete with failure, we map out the terrain of our complicity with the familiar. In sanctuary, we lose our habituated senses of the normal. Perhaps then, in paroxysms of messianic and monstrous promise, we speak with new tongues. This is how the "new" sprouts: not in declarations of righteousness, not in manifestos of the Great New Societies we have intentions of building, not in the stentorian calls for justice. But in the soft places, at the crossroads where bodies meet, in the exilic now, where the fugitive can very suddenly—and oh what a welcome surprise this is!—sense a new color.

•

•

The task is not to abandon identity politics.
The task is to free it to become something stranger.

•

•

Sometimes the image, built from the stories we tell about the world, becomes our prison.

Sometimes the stories we tell about how the world works—who the villains are, who the victims are, who held the abusive whip and who received the lashes, who the plot serves and who it kicks to the precipice—become so territorial, predictable, and fixed, like a forest converted into a park, overlaid with maps, signposts, and little histories entombed at the entrances of its paths, that we fall trapped into the convenience of habit, impervious to the fact that even landscapes travel.

The image freezes us, desensitizes us to little molecular happenings, the little intra-corporeal exchanges here and there, the places where things slip away from their design, the upending of long-established roles and queering of anticipatory models. *Impossible headlines.* A patriarchy of women. The flu becomes a cure for cancer. A capitalist arrangement somehow opens up a space of sacred prayer around slave bones and trinkets rediscovered in the heart of urban Brazil. The presumably innocent domestic abuse activist abuses her powerful husband, and leans on the exoskeleton of the mass media to champion the familiar narratives of unidirectional violence. A slum of white bodies in South Africa. A god travels with his enslaved people across the Atlantic—instead of saving them from their captors. An expected messiah is incarcerated by the ones that await him. "Reality" constantly evades categoricity, refusing to track neatly to our story beats, the patterns and causes we swear by.

In those moments when we *refuse* to budge; when we frown on the arrhythmic cacophonies of the outrageous that interrupt the music we know, the beats we are already dancing to; when we tell ourselves that justice demands unyielding continuity, that a slightly different conception might overthrow the entire edifice of arrival; that we stick to the stories we are used to, and that we stay the course and mow the lawns and clear the weeds and maintain the image—then we begin to eat up ourselves, to subjugate ourselves, to become the very thing we say the "other" is. Because we are never well-practiced in thinking processually, in thinking about the ways the master's rape of the slave endangers the categoricity of his mastery and feeds a wider ecology of intra-becoming that will not be storied into neat binaries—because we will need the security of the usual, we will often be quarantined away from the unusual, from the potentially emancipatory politics of the peripheral.

In those times, the thing to do—if we are so enabled and gifted by the crippling agency of the trickster, might be to stay with the tensions of duplicity. To listen when it would be easier to talk. To sit with the shock of the caricature where one seeks the affirmation of the habitual image, for the caricature is how the image lets down its hair and breathes.

Yes, the caricature is the image's secret refusal to abide faithfully by our conceptions of the world. Oh! that we might hear the secret invitation of the distorted.

•

•

For many, the apocalypse is the messianic disruption of history, the blast just down the heavy road. Going forward is out of the question. For others, the apocalypse is Tuesday. The eddies of loss and the hieroglyphics of death imprinted on marked bodies. The legacies of excavation. The feeling of having one's face pressed to the ground so forcefully that the dirt cleans our skin. The troubling incertitude that does not know time as a tarmac luxuriously dotted with expertise and strategic foresight. The wisdom that has learned to shrug its shoulders when asked: "What is your five-year plan?" For these ones, the world is not about to end. For these ones "climate justice" looks like an extension of whiteness. For these ones, the "messiah," the disruption so anxiously delayed by the prayers of propertied humans, never left for the heavens. The messianic descended into hell and made good company, dancing drunk with kin at the feet of worlds that have ended many times before.

•

•

I have often taken issue with the dominant ways "healing," "well-being," "justice," and even the Jungian-inspired "integration" are popularly deployed to suggest that a self can summarily achieve (and is entitled to) some kind of totalizing resolution, or can arrive at a psychic singularity or unity of sorts that smooths out the creases of subjectivity into a tolerable uniformity.

The implied promises of some of these healing approaches are, for instance, in the discourse on trauma, that one can "heal" one's intergenerational trauma (all of it, some insist, if "you do the work well"), and that the embodied ideal of a good life is encapsulated in being "well," which, to translate, means one is largely free of our psychic dramas (imbalances? disturbances?).

But if this were possible, if one could be fully realized and balanced ... if one could be "well" in this unexamined, absolutizing sense, entirely or progressively free from the psychic termites that gnaw at the furniture of our experiences, one would have to be alone. But it cuts even deeper than being "alone": "one" would not be possible. This is because selves and bodies are neither resolved nor resolvable.

To be "well" in the sense that some aspire to, one would have to silence and freeze the other lives that are still living with and through us. One would have to travel through all the realms, through times past and times yet to come—like Frigga did to save her son, Balder—and extract an oath from all things, from evolutionary dynamics and fungal secretions and anglerfish and trade winds and railway tracks and microplastic immigrants, forcing them to assert that they'd never move again, that they'd cease to conduct their daily lives. One would have to correct the tilt of the earth's crippled spinning so that it turned straight. It is not simply a matter of scanning for toxic ancestors in one's timeline: ancestry is mostly about contexts and worlds, and not singularly about human forebears.

My sense of things—without prejudice to the situated forms of care that must be articulated against a backdrop of agonistic tensions—is that wellness cannot be had as such, since "life" itself is unwell. This paradigmatic unwellness is the very condition of life's vitality, its spontaneity, its corrosive awkwardness.

The idea that traumas are personological phenomena, bound up neatly in conveniently independent selves, lurking somewhere in isolated bodies, obscures the idea that selves are not still and disconnected from other bodies. Other worlds. Other lives. Other deaths.

The hidden curriculum of contemporary wellness is the systematization of bodies within colonial patterns of settlement. The hidden dynamic of wellness is the proliferation of a necropolitics that swirls in the machine of the Anthropocene.

The alternative to being well is to be in touch.

•

•

A certain strand of anti-humanist thinking lays the blame for climate disruption squarely at the feet of humans. In a volatile nutshell, the core idea of this anti-humanism is this: if humans did not overpopulate the planet, destroy ecosystems, commit atrocious crimes against each other, pump gases into the atmosphere, proliferate plastic products that hurt other species, the earth would be in a better and healthier place. Ergo, the elimination of humans is a good thing. In some extreme instances, we must stop having children (or even curse our own parents for giving birth to us).

Ironically, anti-humanism is emphatically pro-humanism. In the very effort to villainize the figure of the human, it re-prioritizes it and centralizes it. What this approach misses, what it throws away to the background, is that what we conveniently call "human" is an ongoing cartographical project of microbial, geological, gastronomical, political, sociopsychological, scientific, technological, ecological, theological consortia. The idea that humans are discrete biological bodies with prerelational properties and qualities (that are either good or bad) already surgically removes "humans" from their intimate relationships with the world. Perhaps more worryingly, it discountenances the contributions of nonhumans in and around us (you know, like the microbial symbionts that constitute and shape how we think, the moods we have, and the capacities we claim as exclusive to us), paints a rosy picture of "nature" as this harmonious and stable place devoid of violence and pain and loss, and arrives at a resolution too convenient to the old narratives of good versus evil. If all things "human" must go, then what do we do with this human narrative? And if the counterargument is that the narrative is not human, then anti-humanism must at least acknowledge that there are other-than-human agencies that shape the world's materialization—and which render moot the urgency of anti-humanism.

If the affect of guilt reinvests us with an all-or-nothing drive to rid the planet of humans, then anti-humanism is humanism's most intelligent move yet. Discontinuity is often a system's most creative effort at perpetuating itself.

•

•

Democracy works by a seemingly innocent idea: rule by the majority. Let the enlightened citizen decide how they want to live and how they want to be governed. If more people prefer that articulated choice, mount up a government on those principles. One person, one vote. Simple enough. But it has never worked this way mainly because the unit of democratic governance is not "a person" or the rational voter or the innocent vote, but a complicated and heterogeneous network of human and more-than-human processes that includes, among others, the mass media and its influential narrative-shaping biases masked as professional objectivism; the attraction of incumbent power; the huge role of money and the corporate consolidation of agency; the socioeconomic isolation and colonized imagination of the marginalized; the self-referential fragility and performative righteousness of the shamed oppressor class; collective addictions to the myth of the photogenic hero; a loveless technosocial landscape and ethical milieu that sterilizes identity, antagonizes difference, and is unforgiving in its proliferation of sinners; an educational system that privileges the correct answer and linear thinking; the intoxicating tribalism of partisan politics; hope.

In short, democracy is based on the idea that the voter is free. But the voter is neither free nor rational. People will kick and scratch their way out of a conversation about health care and money in politics because they don't like the way a candidate looks. More than rational processes are afoot in an electoral system that only has the algorithm to privilege or produce "rational choices" as an end product. But "choice" is the myth. The voter is an extension of the apparatus. The voter is a concept of the vote. The Vote. And the Vote gains its power by disconnecting the voter from the affective wilds that have always been, and are always implicated, when we vote. The printed page of the ballot is not blank or disinterested; it is already scribbled upon with invisible ink. A palimpsest of hidden scripts. Electoral politics will largely tend to leave things the same, to repeat itself. The more invisible the assemblage is (that is, the more we fail to notice how unfree we are), the more provincial and impoverished our politics will be.

We need a new politics, not by declaration or by violent endings and bloodshed. Not by victory or eloquent manifestos. But by touching the matters the Vote performatively leaves out of view. We need small implosions of messianic im/possibility. Modest reappraisals of the claims and promises of conventional power. And sitting in the dark until something happens.

•

•

The only way to know the world, or to think about the world, is to think with it, to participate with/in it, to intervene, and to make marks upon it—even as those marks are made on our own bodies in the selfsame moment. The idea that there is a place to occupy, a privileged site upon which to perch ourselves and with unbothered feathers look out on the world, a place outside the world that is pure and uncluttered (or perhaps deep within ourselves in its promising interiority) from which we can view everything … a view from nowhere and everywhere at once … is the epistemic affordance of geophysical and colonial stability.

To know is to navigate speciated territories of corporeal exchanges. To know is to become unhinged, to be bruised, to be beaten, to be broken. To know is to be filleted and de-fleshed. It is to have stretch marks penned on the body, the fonts of an encounter, echoes of an obstruction. One does not think without becoming something else.

•

•

Postactivism, the concept that informs my notion of making sanctuary, is a matter of irruptions and eruptions, breakthroughs, cracks, flashes, fissures, fault lines, discontinuities, blasts, splits, rifts, ruptures, seismic shifts, world-ending openings, miracles, strange encounters, and the yawning maw of a monster. It is my way of describing the flows and possibilities that proceed from the moment when things no longer fit.

Let me explain.

In a cetologist's book about meeting with orcas—I would recommend this book if I remembered the title, but I don't: it has been a long time since I read it, but this particular account in the book, faintly recalled, has stayed with me through the years—she describes her routine of visiting the large swimming pool where the killer whales (or was it bottlenose dolphins?) lived as part of an ongoing study of cetacean intelligence. Studying whales was her life's passion. She knew her way around. She knew the rituals, the technologies, the tools, the jargon, the prompts, the data. She knew what to do.

But one day, quite suddenly, she didn't.

She had a session with the beasts, but quickly found out that all her prompts and expectations weren't going according to plan. She issued a command, but there was no usual response. They didn't push the floating ball or do whatever she had requested. Puzzled, she left for the day—only to return to the same confusing phenomenon the next day. And the day after that. She worried about them. However, she did notice that the objects of her lifelong fascination seemed to be making advances towards her in ways that didn't seem remarkable at first, and that they seemed to be conferencing among themselves. One day, it suddenly hit her: they were studying her. Somehow, they had turned the researcher's gaze back on her. The cetologist was now the object of cetacean scrutiny.

I imagine it was near impossible for this biologist to return to the same protocols she was used to. This explosion in the fabric of cetological continuity—when orcas start to meddle with research protocols and mess with data—must have had world-ending repercussions. What do you do when a passive rock, lithic and dumb, sprouts a limb? When a mountain you've been climbing sighs gently? When you are interrupted with the realization that the microbial culture you've been frying in your laboratory might have an internal life, and might feel pain? When a tiny virus wreaks havoc on commodious economies and systems of thought? When the ground beneath our feet thaws in the heat of global warming, withdraws its endorsement of modern perpetuity, and haunts our conversations? What do you do when the world kicks back?

Postactivism is not a superior form of being that guarantees solutions. It is not "post-" in the sense of being a successor narrative, a deeper truth, a surer track to utopian worlds, a formula for saving the world. Instead, it is com-post, the site where continuity becomes impossible and transformation inevitable, where "the world" in its colonizing completeness feels less compelling than that one riven place that sprouts alien notions, and where the solutions of the highway seem inadequate to a now unusual, more-than-human arrangement.

A frothing crack opens in the ground, enacting a break in the seamless totality and knowability of things, disrupting the exclusivity of human agency and inquiry, dispersing vitality, and expanding sociality to include things we hadn't considered. Everything changes, becomes stranger. This is postactivism.

When we have come to the end of the world, and there are no more words.

•

•

this is the sanctuary we need—
the one that knows
when times are urgent
we must slow down

SELAH

•

About the Art

The artwork on the cover and throughout the book are selections and croppings from an ongoing series of works titled *(de)facing*. These portraits begin with a printed image: the recognizable face. This is the face that is grown in sociality, formed through the return and repetition of an articulating public gaze, captured through the representational technology of the photograph. And then, through an act of literal *de-facing*—sanding, scratching, painting over—the surface of the face is disrupted. A space opens to face the world differently.

—Krista Dragomer

BÁYỎ AKÓMOLÁFÉ, PhD, rooted with the Yoruba people in a more-than-human world, is the father to Alethea Aanya and Kyah Jayden Abayomi and the grateful life-partner to EJ, as well as a son and a brother. A widely celebrated international speaker, posthumanist thinker, poet, teacher, self-styled "trans-public" intellectual, and essayist, he is the author of two books: *These Wilds Beyond Our Fences: Letters to My Daughter on Humanity's Search for Home* and *We Will Tell Our Own Story: The Lions of Africa Speak* (with Professors Molefi Kete Asante and Augustine Nwoye). Akómoláfé is the visionary founder of the Emergence Network, a planet-wide networking project and inquiry at the edges of the Anthropocene that seeks to convene new kinds of responsivities, sensuous solidarities, and experimental practices for a posthumanist parapolitics. Akómoláfé currently lectures at Pacifica Graduate Institute in California, and was recently appointed the Hubert Humphrey Distinguished Professor of American Studies at Macalester College in Minnesota (beginning in fall 2025). He is also the inaugural Global Senior Fellow of the Othering and Belonging Institute at the University of California (Berkeley); the inaugural W. E. B. Du Bois Scholar in Residence for Trans-Public Intellectualism at the Schumacher Center for a New Economics; and the inaugural Scholar in Residence for the Aspen Institute. Akómoláfé lives between Chennai, India and Great Barrington, Massachusetts with his family. He considers Brazil to be his spiritual home.

EDEN PEARLSTEIN is a multimedia language-artist and cofounder of Ayin Press. He is the author of *Nothing Is for Everyone: Poems*, a creative contributor to *SURVIVA: A Future Ancestral Field Guide* by Cannupa

Hanska Luger, and coauthor/editor of the chapbook *In/Flux: On Influence, Inspiration, Transmission, and Transformation*. He lives in Philadelphia with his wife and two children.

KRISTA DRAGOMER is a Brooklyn-based artist working in visual art, text, and sound. She is the inaugural Vunja Artist-in-Residence for Báyò Akómoláfé's organization Dancing with Mountains. A selection of her drawings is included in Dr. Beatrice Marovich's *Sister Death: Political Theologies for Living and Dying* and in the forthcoming anthology from For The Wild.

AORA BOOKS is an imprint of Ayin Press that explores transformational thought and culture beyond borders, disciplines, and traditions. The name Aora is a neologism inspired by the Ancient Greek aorist tense, which reflects actions that can exist at various points in time, and the word *aoristos*: "without boundaries." This openness defines Aora's mission: to publish works that forge bold connections across places, times, ideas, and beings often seen as separate. Rooted in polyvocality and planetary consciousness, Aora embraces complexity and interconnection. To make a tax-deductible contribution to our work, visit our website at *www.ayinpress.org/donate*.

www.aorabooks.org
www.ayinpress.org